MW01274063

Through the Valley of the Shadow

WALLY HILD

Diana

I hope you enjoy this story.

Best always

Wally.

© Copyright 2006 Wally Hild.
All rights reserved. No part of this publication may be reproduced, stored in a retrieval
system, or transmitted, in any form or by any means, electronic, mechanical, photocopying,
recording, or otherwise, without the written prior permission of the author.

I'm grateful to our son-in-law Allen Haddrell for creating the front and back cover of this
book and to Ed Andres who took the photograph I used for the back cover. Thank you.

Published by Circle Of Light Publishing
First Printing, December 2005

Note for Librarians: A cataloguing record for this book is available from Library and Archives
Canada at www.collectionscanada.ca/amicus/index-e.html
ISBN 1-4120-7556-4

*Printed in Victoria, BC, Canada. Printed on paper with minimum 30% recycled fibre. Trafford's print shop
runs on "green energy" from solar, wind and other environmentally-friendly power sources.*

Offices in Canada, USA, Ireland and UK
This book was published *on-demand* in cooperation with Trafford Publishing. On-demand
publishing is a unique process and service of making a book available for retail sale to the
public taking advantage of on-demand manufacturing and Internet marketing. On-demand
publishing includes promotions, retail sales, manufacturing, order fulfilment, accounting and
collecting royalties on behalf of the author.

Book sales for North America and international:
Trafford Publishing, 6E–2333 Government St.,
Victoria, BC V8T 4P4 CANADA
phone 250 383 6864 (toll-free 1 888 232 4444)
fax 250 383 6804; email to orders@trafford.com
Book sales in Europe:
Trafford Publishing (UK) Limited, 9 Park End Street, 2nd Floor
Oxford, UK OXI IHH UNITED KINGDOM
phone 44 (0)1865 722 113 (local rate 0845 230 9601)
facsimile 44 (0)1865 722 868; info.uk@trafford.com
Order online at:
trafford.com/05-2451

10 9 8 7 6 5

THIS BOOK IS DEDICATED to Jodi, Chris and Caroline and every one of our family and friends who supported and loved us during this most intense and uncertain time in our lives. It was your thoughts and prayers that guided us through the darkest moments and gave us the courage to continue on. We found out in spades that we have little control over events in our lives but it is how we respond, either positively or negatively to them, that determines the outcome.

Forward

THIS IS THE STORY of Wally Hild's decision to fight to beat the insidious enemy that invades his body, robs him of his vitality and threatens his life.

In his first book "From Hodgkin's to Ironman" we follow the road Wally travels as he overcomes his water phobia to swim Lake Okanagan and his numb bum to complete the cycling challenge up hill and down dale, then with a gimpy knee he tackles the run.

I wept as I watched him drag himself cross the finish line to the incredulous words of the commentator Steve King and the acclamations of the crowd into the waiting arms of his beloved Caroline and his children – an Ironman indeed.

Now in this prequel we are invited to join Wally in his first race, one, which if he lost, meant death. As we follow him from diagnosis through the harrowing treatments with no assurance of the final outcome, we see at work that indomitable spirit that carries him over the finish line in the Ironman competition playing a major role in the outcome.

This is an essential book for all of us.

Not all of us will run the Ironman, not all of us will go from a wheel chair to a medal around our neck, but there is a good chance that we or one of our loved ones will be faced with treatment for a serious illness.

Here, as we journey with Wally through the "Valley of the Shadow", we see how faith, hope, and determination not to quit, leads him through the darkness into the spectacular light of a glorious dawn.

Reverend Dr. Alex Lawson

Acknowledgements

I INITIALLY WANTED TO call this book, Faith, Family and Friends because it was those three elements that were instrumental in how this story played out. One does not achieve anything by oneself, especially when confronted by a life-threatening illness that shakes you to the core. It is at those times that family, friends and whole communities of acquaintances and strangers come forward in support.

To all our family and friends in Penticton, Lethbridge and all the other towns and cities across the country who held us in their prayers and thoughts of healing, we are grateful. Many showed up at our doorstep to provide morale uplifting. It's amazing how God works by sending those to become part of one's healing. For me, many people have been woven in to the fabric of my life's tapestry.

I'm fortunate to have met and have been taught how to write by the four founding members of the Penticton Writers and Publishers who were so helpful and supportive of my two books. They are Janelle Breeze-Biagioni, Lorraine Pattison, Penny Smith and Yasmine Thorpe.

Thanks to every one at the Bank of Montreal who've been so unwavering in their support for me and especially Caroline. They've included her in all functions, inside and outside work, after her stroke in 2000.

I'm sincerely grateful to the Canadian Cancer Society, locally and provincially and the oncology doctors and staff in Vancouver who were integrated into this scenario.

To Drs. Jeff and Leona Harries, Dr. Keith McIvor and all the medical professionals in Penticton who treated me with the upmost care and respect; your collective expertise was one of the major reasons I survived.

I am thankful to all the staff of Oncology at Penticton Regional Hospital who became more than care providers. They became friends to all of us. They are acknowledged in this book.

And I'm especially grateful for the opportunity to have been at the right place at the right time to have met and been treated by Dr. Jack Chritchley. He was at the vortex of those in medicine who surrounded my family and me with such caring, allowing me a second chance at life.

Jack transcended the traditional role of healer to become my friend. I will forever be grateful for his kindness, gentleness, humour and his astounding medical abilities. He went far beyond his job description for not just me, but every patient who was referred to him.

Here's to you Jack.

Thanks.

Chapter 1

It was the 60's.

Growing up as a teenager in Calgary, Alberta was exciting as we drag-raced our old anemic small-block Chevys from stoplight to stoplight through the downtown intersections on Saturday nights. Sometimes other lights, the bubble gum machine-shaped red lights on black cars with white doors, spoiled our fun. After a stern lecture from a sober-faced cop, we found less populated streets to continue our racing.

Life was easy. My handful of car-nut friends and I lived day to day, without responsibility to guide us. Decisions were made moment to moment, by the seat of our pants, lacking thought and consequence. We could not comprehend tomorrow.

One hot August night in the middle of the month in 1968, at a quarter to midnight, Rick Elvey and Dave Sidwell, whom I'd known since tenth grade, stopped in at the Edmonton Trail Esso where I pumped gas and did oil changes. I'd been working part-time through the weekends and summers throughout high school and was on full time staff since graduation two months earlier.

Dave rolled down the passenger window of the winged brown and white 1959 Impala sedan owned by Rick as the car came to a screeching halt in front of the first open door of the four bay service area. I'd just finished changing the oil on a '66 Mustang convertible. He yelled out, "hey Hild – watcha doin' at midnight?"

"Why?"

"We're going to California tonight. Wanna come?"

As I wiped my hands on a rag and hit the switch to lower the hydraulic hoist holding the Ford, the loud, hissing noise of escaping air as it slowly lowered to the floor made me shout back my answer.

"I CAN'T GO WITH YOU GUYS. I GOTTA BE BACK HERE AT EIGHT IN THE MORNING". The car's tires touched the concrete floor and the noise died out.

"We don't care", Rick shot back as he leaned over Dave's shoulder. "We'll be back in fifteen minutes. You decide".

I could tell by the mischievous grin on his face he wasn't kidding.

At midnight, I jumped into the wide back seat of his car, still wearing my jeans, sneakers and light-blue, slightly soiled Esso work shirt. I weakly protested that it was a stupid idea. Rick nosed the '59 Chevy out of the service station lot, pointed the car west on 16ᵗʰ Avenue and hit the accelerator. Our destination was Banff, then west to Vancouver and south on Interstate 5 to paradise.

"Wanna change?" Dave asked from the passenger seat. "You stink".

He pointed to a bag on the floorboards behind Dave. We were all about the same height and weight. They'd quickly thrown together a bunch of shorts, cut-off jeans, T-shirts and some footwear consisting of sandals and tennis shoes.

I truly questioned my sanity and mused aloud about the change of clothing and *how the hell are we gonna pay for food and where are we gonna sleep?*

That chilling thought suddenly made me sit up straight.

"Hey! How much money have you guys got?", I blurted out as we streaked out of the city limits. "I've only got a few bucks and my Esso credit card". They both laughed.

Rick said, "My cousin is a stewardess. She lives in Marina del Rey and she's never home. She said we could crash at her apartment but only if we sleep on the balcony. That's why we brought some sleeping bags. They're in the trunk."

"Money...money...MONEY...boys – we need money to buy food and gas", I protested loudly. They said they had a hundred and ten dollars, some of it saved, some borrowed... and I didn't want to know where they got the rest.

"How much have YOU got?" Rick asked, looking at me through the rear view mirror. I reached into my jeans and pulled out three crumpled ones and a couple of quarters.

"A hundred and thirteen bucks is NOT gonna get us to California and BACK", I yelled, my annoyance making my voice rise.

"We kinda thought...maybe...maybe...we could put... ah...the gas...on your card", Rick stuttered.

"OH WE DID, DID WE? WHEN DID WE DECIDE TO USE MY CREDIT CARD?" It sunk in. I'd been had. "YOU SET ME UP DIDN'T YOU – YOU LOW LIFE SONS OF BITCHES!" I shrieked.

They put their hands over their mouths and I could hear them trying to silence their snickering. When they finished their full-blown guffaws, they promised to pay me back when we were home again. If we weren't thundering down the TransCanada Highway at 75 miles an hour, I think I would've jumped out.

Thirty-six hours later, on Friday afternoon, we arrived in Hawthorne, California, the birthplace of the Beach Boys. Our pilgrimage had both ended and begun. En route, we'd passed all the beaches we'd heard about in the surf and car songs while growing up in the frozen great white north.

Redondo. Manhattan. Long Beach. Rincon.

That night after the sun had set and we'd rolled out our sleeping bags on the third floor balcony of Rick's cousin's apartment overlooking the million dollar yachts at Marina del Rey, we drove back to Manhattan Beach.

"Last one in's a dork!" Rick yelled as he rolled out the

driver's door and hit the sand running. He'd slammed the gearshift into 'park' before the car stopped. I bolted out of the back door, the car still rolling like a boat on rough water. I raced down the hundred yards from the parking lot to the surf, tearing off my clothes.

Just as I got to the water, I stumbled as my right leg became snarled by the flapping pants. I did a face-plant in the waterlogged sand and the salty taste permeated my lips. I heard Rick and Dave screaming out in laughter as they hit the surf, buck-naked and dove in. I fumbled with my jeans and soon I too, was frolicking and splashing in the warm ocean as millions of drops of water, reflecting in the full moon, sprayed around us.

We were delirious with joy. Three stubble-jumping prairie kids were living a dream in that steamy California night.

The next morning I decided to call home and let my mom know where I was.

"Hi", I said as cheerfully as I could, pretending as if nothing was out of the ordinary.

"Where are you?", she queried, not seemingly too concerned.

I was known to spend the night at a friend's home without letting her know.

Perhaps she thought that was the case with the phone call.

"Ah…ah…I'm…ah…we're…um…we'reinsouthernCalifrnia" I blurted out in one breath – which I held, expecting a verbal spanking from the other end.

There was a long pregnant pause. I could feel my heart pounding in my temples.

"How long will you be?"

How cool was that!

I travelled fifteen hundred miles, after walking away from my job without telling my boss and my mom asks how long I'm gonna be.

"No more than a month", I quickly assured her. I told her I loved her and hung up.

The sixties for me was played out in 24 hour increments. I looked no further ahead than one day at a time. I had no responsibilities, a job whenever I wanted one, a few good friends and was thoroughly enjoying life.

Future was what parents planned for. What did it matter to me?

I hadn't even decided what I might do for the rest of my life since leaving high school. I had several choices. Drive truck. Work in construction. Go to university.

Because I was quite athletic during high school, I had thoughts of perhaps becoming a physed teacher. I'd played a year of high school football and had been involved with hockey since I was seven years old.

Jobs were plentiful and my needs were few. All I desired was to earn enough money to buy gas for my car, the odd pizza and beer.

One thought which barely surfaced in my mind during those heady and giddy days was contemplating the effects of a life-threatening disease. *That's only for old, sick people* I'd think whenever I'd heard or read about those who'd succumbed because of illness.

Even the death of my father two years earlier didn't trigger the possibility that I might one day have to face my own mortality. He had passed away after a lengthy battle with lung cancer and my mind had unconsciously short-circuited any thoughts that I may one day have to journey in his footsteps. I was having way too much fun enjoying my days as a wanna-be, bleached hair, pseudo-hippy on my magical mystery tour.

After we returned from our California adventure, I worked for two years in the warehouse at Western Grocers. My job was loading and unloading groceries from semi-trailer trucks and rail cars. Summer heat and winter cold coupled with backbreaking labor made me quickly decide that real work was not for me. As a result I enrolled at the Southern Alberta

Institute of Technology in their Television, Stage and Radio Arts Program. I began my broadcasting career in September of 1971 in Peace River, Alberta where I spent a lot of time at work and little effort on my physical well-being by neglecting a good diet and boycotting the gym. My weight increased dramatically.

I came to my senses, however in 1974, two years after marrying my high school sweetheart, Caroline Blackburn. I regained my high school football physique and weight of about 160 pounds after having ballooned to 195 because of too much pizza, beer and inactivity.

Punching buttons and pushing sliders on an electronic control board and turntables in a radio station did not contribute to me becoming a world-class athlete. I remember the day I made the decision to change my shape after taking a long look at myself in a mirror. I was disgusted with what I saw. My former 32 inch waist had exploded to 38. My suit jackets were size 44 – and I was only five feet nine inches tall.

My old jeans hung forlornly in the closet. My shirts did not fit anymore. I had to buy longer belts. Looking down, I couldn't see if I was wearing sneakers or loafers. My feet had disappeared below the expanse of my belly and I knew what I had to do.

I saw a doctor and after a routine physical and questions about my life-style, he told me there was nothing wrong with me that getting back into shape wouldn't correct.

The following day I bought a new pair of runners and set out that evening after work. I ran around my block and nearly passed out at the back door when I got home. Caroline helped me to the kitchen table and handed me a glass of water. I gulped it in one swallow. The tomatoes she'd picked from our garden that afternoon were only slightly more red than my face. My lungs were on fire. Even though I didn't smoke, I coughed constantly as I inhaled lungfuls of air with a raspy wheeze. I chugged two more glasses of water.

Great, isn't it I thought. *I'll be exercising in the house too as I run to the bathroom several times in the middle of the night – every night.*

From that day on, I increased my distance by one side of a city block every time I ran. I maintained my fitness over the following twenty years by weight training, cycling, hockey and climbing the ladder in broadcasting.

Caroline and I spent the 1970's and 80's putting our lives together. After signing a life-long mortgage, we began to raise our two children, son Christopher and daughter Jodi. Leaving my carefree youth behind, my life was on track. We both had good jobs, she in banking and me in radio and television. We lived in Lethbridge, Alberta for 17 years after having spent the previous five years in several cities around the province gaining experience in our careers. Our children grew up from kindergarten to high school with the same friends they'd known since childhood.

Then, suddenly and without warning, like the Chinook winds that blow through southern Alberta, we moved on Remembrance Day, 1993 leaving behind relatives and life-long friends. I'd been offered a new job in a new province. Our future seemed secure and on course with life promising to be just as wonderful in Penticton, British Columbia, 525 miles west of Lethbridge.

The nagging, ongoing middle back pains which had surfaced a few months earlier, had become annoying but I'd told myself the move would prove I was still in great physical shape. I'd been pushing weights for several years and attributed the soreness to being injured in the gym. However, lifting heavy boxes, a fridge, sofa and asundry of other household items was much more difficult than I imagined. I struggled as I attempted to help friends and family load up the rented 2-ton moving van, trying to convince myself the pain would ease as we got settled into our new home in B.C.

Tearfully, we said our goodbyes to our loved ones in

Alberta, hugged our hugs, kissed our kisses and began a new chapter in our lives.

We left early Thanksgiving morning in our car, followed by our friend Ernie Joly who was driving the moving van. He was accompanied by Corey Thibert, son of long-time friends Rome and Carol. The late fall weather was perfect until we got into the Rockies where heavy snow in the Rogers Pass area west on the TransCanada Highway slowed us to a crawl at times.

Twelve hours later we arrived in the Okanagan Valley and unpacked at our rented duplex up the eastern hills of Penticton. We had spent a weekend in the Peach City a month-and-a-half earlier searching for a home after accepting a sales position at CIGV FM offered by owner Ralph Robinson. We'd decided not to buy a house for a few months until we became familiar with our new city.

As we unloaded the truck, I became increasingly alarmed as I found myself tiring very easily, not able to get my second wind. As I had done so many times before over the previous half-year, I shrugged off the aches and discomfort which were becoming more intense and frequent. The pain did not go away as quickly as it did in the past when I was exercising too much or too hard.

It was irritating and I started to swing between anger and fear. Anger, because I didn't feel strong and well, and fear because I sensed something was dreadfully wrong and I was afraid to face the uncertainty head-on. I sensed an awful shadow; a sinister knawing at the base of my spine that signaled an ominous foreboding and I knew I had to see a doctor.

But like so many things in life, I was too busy to do what I should have done.

I'd embraced my new job at the radio station and wanted to do well. I promised myself I would make a medical appointment after we'd adjusted to our new home and lifestyle.

Christmas 1993 found us in Salmon Arm with my brother

Wolf, his wife Corine and their teenagers Heather and Ryan. It was the first time in the twenty years since they moved from Calgary that our families had celebrated the holidays together.

The intensifying back pain took away my joy. On Christmas Eve, the nagging, irritating discomfort took a disconcerting and violent turn. As we sat down to dinner, a sudden, shooting pain rocketed through my right hip. It felt as if a red-hot poker had been thrust into my pelvis. I winced in pain and asked Corine if she had any extra-strength pain relievers.

Then suddenly, as quickly as it struck, the searing jolt disappeared. I was sweating profusely. I told everyone what had happened. Caroline looked at me, worried and asked how I felt. I got up and walked around the kitchen for a couple of minutes.

"I'm okay", I lied.

But I knew, deep inside, I had experienced the beginning of something that would take me to an unknown and uncertain future. The hair on the back of my neck stood up as I felt a true, horrifying fear – that of the unknown.

After the holidays and through the typically dreary, cloudy and rainy wintery Okanagan days, I continued as best as I could with my fitness regime. Caroline and I took a walk every evening after supper for as long as my legs would take me. My mind kept telling me *you'll be okay if you keep yourself in shape...gotta keep moving...can't let down...it's gotta get better.*

Six weeks after Christmas, the incidents of stabbing pain increased and intensified, centering in my right hip and often caused me to wake up at night. Trying to cope with the discomfort, I hadn't taken anything more powerful than the over-the-counter pain killers at first. I finally asked Caroline for her Tylenol 3's with codeine which she took occasionally for her chronic back pain. They gave me some relief and I always kept several pills with a glass of water on the night table beside my bed.

Then, late one night around the middle of January, the night sweats began.

Nothing can adequately describe the condition. I'd heard of them but had never paid attention because I hadn't thought I'd ever become a victim.

They initially attacked while I was sleeping. The combination of intense cold and drenching sweat left me chilled and shaking until I took a couple of pills. Ten minutes later, I would feel warm again and could go back to sleep. Gradually though, over the following few weeks, the condition worsened. I was held hostage by a real-life, creeping, Stephen King horror novel manifesting itself within me. The freezing cold in my spine was so intense at times, I'd crawl under Caroline to try to warm up. She held me tight, forcing me deeper into our waterbed which had been turned up to 100 Fahrenheit.

I wished in the middle of this freezing hell, I could be enveloped in a soothing hot gel which would comfort me and deliciously warm me up. I shook uncontrollably. My teeth chattered like a jackhammer. I could barely pick up the painkillers with my shaking right hand. Sometimes, I'd drop them because I couldn't control my fingers. I usually slept without clothing but was forced to dress in sweat pants and T-shirts. After each night sweat I peeled off my soaked apparel, towelled off and put on dry clothes. We also had to change our bedsheets.

When the sweats were very intense, I could run my index finger along the center of my rib cage and surf in the perspiration from my throat to my belly button.

In the darkness of the midnight hour, it all seemed surreal; the pain, clammy wetness, then relief when the pain killers kicked in. I was living an out-of-control nightmare; one that sucked the energy from me and left my body drained and exhausted in the morning. Sometimes during the day, the hip pain would strike me at the office or when I was on a sales call. I began to sweat and my teeth chattered and experienced the uncomfortable, sticky sensation of wet shirt on my skin. That led to more shakes because the outside temperature was around freezing.

Through hollowed, darkened eyes each morning, I saw a haggard-looking face staring back in fear at me from the bathroom mirror. My weight had slowly dropped from my frame, like leaves from a tree in late autumn. It wasn't noticeable at first. Then my shirts became too big. My enormous appetite was gone and I didn't feel like eating. My pants hung from my hips like drapes. One evening I stepped on the scale. My eyes widened in horror as the numbers on the rotation dial whirled around and slowly stopped.

I looked at myself in the mirror. The blood drained from my face and my legs turned to jelly. I steadied myself on the bathroom counter and slowly, with apprehension and fear, looked down again at the scale.

144 pounds! I knew I had to see a doctor.

Dr. Jeff Harries was recommended to me by one of the people at the radio station.

I made the appointment the following day. Two days later, he was interviewing me in his clinic. He's a big man, about 6'2" with the frame of a former football linebacker. My illness caused me to look like an apparition when I stood next to him.

As I answered his probing questions, I saw his brow begin to furrow. He appeared more and more concerned with my answers as I detailed the symptoms. He immediately arranged for me to go to a local laboratory to have my blood and urine analyzed.

Twenty-four hours later, I took the elevator instead of the steps to the third floor lab, downtown. Weak and scared, I didn't have the strength to climb the stairs, which, a few months earlier, I would have bounded up, two at a time.

I met with Jeff again two days later in his office. He entered with a file in his hand and sat down, facing me. For a couple of tension-filled minutes, he read through some of the papers in his hands, his eyes, behind his glasses, scanning the information.

I became increasingly nervous. Finally, he put the file in his lap and looked up at me. His eyes focused on mine and in a warm, slow delivery told me the blood tests indicated there was something going on inside me which wasn't good. He told me he was referring me immediately to a local specialist. He continued, "your white blood counts are way up. That indicates something is out of whack". He said I would get a call to confirm my appointment at the office of the other doctor. I thanked Jeff, got up and left the examination room. I walked slowly down the hallway to the front door, my mind spinning.

It was Tuesday afternoon, February 15th. The sky was overcast. A light drizzle fell as I walked to the curb and around the front of my car. A violent shiver suddenly erupted within me. I quickly unlocked the door and got in. I started the car and put the heater on full blast and drove home.

The following afternoon, I left the office for home to try and force some lunch into me. I had a bowl of soup and a cheese sandwich. I'd put on my shoes and trenchcoat and was on my way to the door when the phone rang. I looked at my watch. It was 12:37 p.m.

"Is this Mr. Hild?", a female voice asked after I answered the call.

"Yes"

"This is Pat from oncology to let you know you have an appointment with Dr. Jack Chritchley next Monday afternoon at 3 o'clock. Can you be here?"

"Sure", I said. I asked her to hold for a moment while I got a piece of paper and pencil to jot down the information.

I'd never heard the term 'oncology' before and asked what it meant.

Her answer exploded into my brain and froze that moment forever in my mind.

"Oncology?" She paused for a moment and softly replied, "that's…uh…that's the cancer clinic".

Chapter 2

IT SEEMED LIKE AN eternity had passed since those words ricocheted around the inside of my head.

"Cancer clinic"

Like the streaking steel balls in a brightly lit machine at the arcade, they caromed through my brain and slammed into my heart like a lightning bolt.

Equally as stunning was my response to those two words. I found myself surprisingly calm, with an intense feeling of serenity. No panic. No emotion. Just peace.

It was not at all how I envisioned I would respond to a life-threatening illness.

Breaking down in tears, I thought, would be a more natural reaction to such devastating news.

Cancer...I have cancer. So this is what has caused the night sweats, pain and weight loss.

The strange, silent calmness continued to surround me – an indescribable feeling of absolute peace. I felt the very hand of God softly cradling itself around me. I remember standing there, like a statue, the moment forever solidified, etched in my mind like a work in bronze. The sensation seemed to last for eons, but only moments had passed. I blinked my eyes and reality crashed around me.

I slowly walked from the kitchen into the living room and sat down on the footstool by the recliner, my overcoat spilling around me on the floor. I stared into nothing. The sunshine from the south facing windows had invaded the space where I was slouched. Tiny dust particles, illuminated by the bright rays danced in the air.

A myriad of thoughts pounded into my consciousness. I thought back to the times I buried my parents several years apart. My mortality surfaced at those moments, but only briefly. Now I was forced to look squarely into the abyss of my own possible demise.

A scene from Charles Dickens 'A Christmas Carol' flashed into my mind.

Ebenezer Scrooge was confronted by the Spirit of Christmas yet to come. Face-to-face with his own gravestone, he fell on it and cried out, "Spirit, is it too late for me?"

I saw a vision of Caroline, Jodi and Chris softly crying and clutching each other tightly as they stood near my coffin.

MY DEATH. Could it be my life was to end around that heartbreaking scene, my loved ones suffering so much?

With a sudden jolt of fear and anguish, I quickly gave my head a shake as if to try to fling the horrifying picture from my mind. The image was far too painful, too intense.

Even though I realized I wasn't afraid to die, I was terrified for my family.

My belief in God and the salvation of Jesus Christ gave me the promise of eternal life, but I had so much to do, so much to live for. I wanted to be with Caroline when we had our mortgage burning ceremony, to play hockey again with Chris and to kick a soccer ball with Jodi. I wanted to live to hold our first grandchild. Thoughts of restoring my antique Chevy and driving it again on summer weekends crashed into my head. I remembered seeing the dormant rose bush just outside the front window when I came home and wanted to smell the flowers in full bloom in the spring. I desired to drink in the beauty of the Okanagan Valley and never take a tree for granted again.

There were so many things I wanted to experience for the

first time. Death was not one of them. Time had stood still as I pondered the avalanche of thoughts and feelings.

I felt a chill rise up my spine. I stood up, walked back into the kitchen and took two more Tylenol 3's. I drove back to the office but couldn't concentrate on my work.

All I kept thinking was *how am I going to tell Caroline and the kids that we're facing cancer?*

I spent the afternoon at my desk in a fog, mechanically leafing through the yellow pages looking for potential clients which I often did when I wasn't on sales calls.

At 4:30 I pulled up at the back door of the Bank Of Montreal where Caroline worked as a part-time teller. She'd been with the bank in a full-time capacity since 1974 and was waiting for the opportunity to move into a similar position in Penticton.

A jumble of statements tumbled through my mind. *Honey, I have some bad news.*

No, I'd better not do it that way. *Caroline, please try not to cry.* No, not that way either.

How am I going to tell her I probably have cancer? I was afraid to say anything because she was such an emotional person. My heart was torn apart. I bit my lip and tried to hold back my tears. I remembered when my dad told my mom he'd been diagnosed with lung cancer. The sheer look of terror, hopelessness, despair and anxiety on her face, was one I'll never forget.

What would Caroline's response be?

I'd waited only five minutes when she left the back door of the bank,briskly walked through the blustery winter wind, opened the door and got in. She took one look at me and her usual cheerfulness instantly vanished. She knew something was dreadfully wrong. I gave her a kiss and told her about the phone call four hours earlier. As I explained I was to meet with a specialist in a couple of days, tears welled up in her blue eyes. However, she didn't cry out loud as I though she might.

That moment began her transformation. I knew she had suspected I was very ill, but she tried not to show her fear. Her metamorphosis to becoming a solid, steady rock had begun. She would have to anchor our family as we were thrust into a violent storm for which we were not prepared.

She reached up and placed my haggard, scared face in her gentle hands and when she put her lips to mine, the tears mixed when our cheeks touched. I reached out and pulled her close to me and we hugged, oblivious to what was going on outside. I wasn't conscious of anything around us. I didn't hear the cold wind whistle through the naked trees on the boulevard a few feet away from the car.

After a few minutes, she put on a smile and said, "don't worry, everything is going to be alright". I tried to be reassured by what she was telling me. We looked at each other and realized there was one more very difficult task ahead of us. We had to tell Jodi and Chris.

We arrived home ten minutes later and didn't see Chris' car in the gravel driveway of our duplex. I was hoping they weren't home from school because I wanted some time to compose myself before we sat down to tell them the news. Chris was 17 and in grade twelve, 15 year-old Jodi was in the tenth. They both attended Penticton Secondary High School.

Our kids came home a half-hour later, bounding in the front door just as Caroline was putting supper on the table. After saying our usual grace, I cleared my throat and told them what had transpired. When I mentioned the probable cancer fight ahead, they became very quiet. After a few minutes, Jodi asked me why this was happening.

I thought, *yea, hadn't we uprooted ourselves only months before and moved away from everything that was familiar and comfortable into a strange and unknown environment? Wasn't life supposed to be much better?* I told her I didn't know.

We ate the rest of our supper, mostly in silence, each of us picking away at our food. They asked a couple more questions about what would happen next but I didn't have any answers. I tried to reassure them that nothing had been diagnosed yet and that we had to stay as positive as we could until I met with the cancer specialist.

I went to bed that night wishing Monday would never come.

Chapter 3

THE SUNDAY BEFORE MY appointment at oncology, I drove the CIGV radio van to the eastern outskirts of Penticton. I'd been asked to do an on-location remote broadcast from noon to 4 p.m. at the open house of a new energy-efficient home constructed by a local builder.

The schedule called for me to do four, 60 second commercials each hour, inviting listeners to drop in for coffee and donuts and to chat with the sales representatives.

Things went well for 45 minutes and for the first time in many weeks, I really enjoyed myself, smiling and talking with the visitors. The snacks were also a pleasant treat for me and I indulged in more than just a couple of donuts.

Then all of a sudden, as I started the last break in the first hour, I felt a 'sweat' coming on. Mustering all of the professionalism my 23 years of broadcasting could provide, I strained to finish. It was 'live commercial' radio. I didn't have the luxury of turning off my microphone and playing a record. I couldn't say *I'll be back after these messages.*

My teeth started to chatter as I talked about the benefits of R-60 insulation in the ceiling and R-40 in the walls. It was weird. It felt as if someone was over-riding control of my jaws. I bit down hard on my molars and finished the commercial speaking through my teeth. I clenched them tightly so the clicking porcelain could not be heard by the listener.

I was freezing when I finished and had started to shake.

There were a dozen people just a few feet away from me in the large, luxurious living room. They were too busy talking with the sales reps and builder to take any notice of my condition. I reached into my sports jacket for the small container of Tylenol 3's.

Silently I congratulated myself for concealing my difficulty in speaking. I looked at my watch. It read 12:50 p.m. I had fifteen minutes to recuperate after the news at one o'clock before the first spot in the second hour.

25 minutes to get rid of the sweats.

I left as inconspicuously as I could and quickly walked to the station vehicle. I started the engine and switched on the heater. It took a couple of minutes to fully warm up and soon the heat and drugs took away the shakes and sweats.

As I sat in the car, I relived the sixty seconds of live on-air work and concluded it was almost the most difficult thing I'd ever done in broadcasting. Even more trying than the time I chugged a can of Pepsi, seconds before a live weathercast on 2&7 Lethbridge Television a few years earlier. The suppression of stomach gas for more than five minutes was a monumental task.

The following afternoon at 2:45, Monday February 21, 1994, I arrived at the cancer clinic at the Penticton Regional Hospital for my appointment with Dr. Jack Chritchley, the medical oncologist.

The clinic, tucked away in a corner of the hospital on the main floor, was small but bright, with a large illuminated aquarium against the far wall across from the receptionist's desk. Under one of the two windows to the left of the aquarium was a small table littered with pieces of a puzzle. The center of it showed a castle taking shape. Several empty chairs were situated around the waiting room.

I introduced myself to Pat, the receptionist. I was able to put a face to the call from just a few days ago. She was friendly, with a warm smile that made me feel more at ease and asked me to fill in the blanks of a new patient form. She then invited me to sit down and wait with a couple of people who were already seated, each reading a magazine.

I picked up an ancient copy of National Geographic and mechanically turned the pages not really reading or seeing anything but a blur of colors and text. My mind was on something more pressing. I'd lost track of time when Pat suddenly appeared next to my chair.

"Please follow me, Wally", she requested.

We walked the half-dozen steps down the corridor to an upright scale. I stepped on it and Pat read the number.

"144 pounds"

"Almost twenty pounds under my normal weight", I quietly replied as I stared at the device. I added, "my clothes and shoes probably weight another couple of pounds".

The icy coldness of horror again slowly rose in my spine as my gaze continued to be glued to the numbers at my feet. I mentally deducted two pounds. The chill in my back intensified.

I probably weighed 142 pounds. I stood transfixed. I could not remember the last time I was that light. Perhaps in junior high school.

"Pardon?" I asked. Pat had gently placed her hand on my elbow.

She again asked me to stand up straight so she could measure my height. After also noting it for my records, she led me to Claire Davidson's office, who was the head of oncology nursing.

Near the window opposite the door, was a large bookshelf with dozens of texts and pamphlets with information about patients dealing with cancer. On her desk was a computer and stacks of paper. Pat invited me to sit in a chair to the right of the desk and asked me to wait.

I slumped down, took a deep breath, and winced. That was the first time I realized how sore my chest really was. I slowly exhaled until my lungs were completely empty. I closed my eyes and tried to concentrate on staying as calm as I could.

Question after question bombarded my fatigued mind.

"What's going to happen next?" *"How will they determine what I'm suffering from?"*. Round and round the queries kept rebounding through my brain.

"Are you Wally?"

I opened my eyes and a smiling, bespectacled face greeted me.

"Hi, I'm Claire Davidson. I want to spend a few minutes with you before I introduce you to Dr. Chritchley". She was the first of many medical professionals whom I would meet over the following few weeks. Claire asked if I had any questions.

"Only a zillion", I replied with a half-hearted laugh. She chuckled.

One of my first concerns was my weight loss. I asked her how to counteract it.

She said she wouldn't have an answer until the illness was diagnosed.

She paused for a moment, lowered her voice and in a sympathetic, but matter-of-fact tone said, "you know you're here because we suspect you have some kind of cancer". I nodded and she continued. "Until we know exactly what we're dealing with, we won't get into the specifics of what kind of therapy or therapies Dr. Chritchley might prescribe. I'm not even going to speculate at this point, so when we know, we can talk about treatments, okay?" Again I nodded.

I told her I still had a ton of questions, which needed answers. She reiterated that we'd address them at the appropriate time and added we'd be seeing a lot of each other. I felt good being in her company and I looked forward to speaking with her again.

We got up and she led me into a small room, two doors down the corridor. I thanked her and she closed the door behind her. I looked around me. The room was simple in its décor with an examining table near the only window, a stool and a couple of chairs.

I sat down in the chair closest to the window and rested my head against the wall.

I drifted away to the soothing drone of the heating system overhead.

I wonder if I have to go through chemotherapy?

I'd seen pictures of people who'd lost their hair because of the chemical treatment. A vision of my bald head formed starkly in my mind.

Boy, do I look goofy.

"Good afternoon. I'm Dr. Jack Chritchley."

I snapped back to reality. I was so engrossed with the mental picture of my hairless head, I hadn't heard him open the door and enter the room.

He had a smile on his face as he introduced himself in a soft, low voice accentuated with an easygoing tone.

I stood up, shook his hand and told him my name.

His grip was firm, yet gentle and I felt comforted in his presence. He was dressed in a light blue shirt with a dark tie and was wearing his white clinical smock. A stethoscope dangled around his neck. In his left hand was a clipboard filled with papers.

Dr. Chritchley was a couple of inches taller than me, about 5'11", with graying hair and weighed about 160 pounds. His dark eyes behind his glasses seemed to be compassionate, something I'd expected from a cancer doctor. He appeared quite fit with a healthy complexion. Over the following months I would realize we had much in common. He was quite athletic, and among other activities, enjoyed hiking and hockey.

"I hear you're not doing so well", he volunteered.

I sighed, "No. I certainly have felt better."

I gave him a brief history about our move to the Okanagan and how the pain in my hip, chest and back had intensified over the previous months. We spoke for a couple more minutes and then he proceeded with the examination. He checked my blood pressure, pulse and reflexes. He asked me to remove most of my clothing and I stripped to my shorts.

"Please sit on the edge of the examination table", he asked.

With the deftness that comes from years of practice, he softly kneaded the area around the base of my neck, behind the collarbones then to the top of the neck and around the regions under my eyes. As his fingers searched, he continually asked about my declining health and I detailed the chills, night sweats and weight loss.

He stopped momentarily and told me in a very undramatic, matter-of-fact approach that he suspected I was suffering from Hodgkin's disease.

"Hodgkin's – isn't that what Mario Lemieux just had?" I asked. I'd read the newspaper accounts and saw the interview on TSN when the Pittsburgh Penguins star was diagnosed with the cancer and had to leave hockey to undergo his radiation treatments.

"Uh-huh", he nodded. "It's the same disease, but his was diagnosed much earlier". He paused for a moment, lowered his voice and said, "you've been ill for a very, very long time. Long before your move here to Penticton".

He asked me to lie down and told me he was going to finish the examination by checking my chest, armpits, lower abdomen and the backs of my knees. He said he was looking for enlarged lymph nodes. We didn't speak much and I found the silence uncomfortable. I was aware of my breathing that seemed to be more shallow and rapid than usual. The soreness in my chest that I had started to feel a few weeks earlier seemed to be more painful as well.

"This may be uncomfortable", he said as he dug his fingers in the soft area in both sides of my groin, just above the pelvic bone. I winced as the kneading of the tender areas caused me to flinch. "Sorry", he said, "but I have to do this".

He concluded his investigation at the backs of my knees and asked me to sit up.

With his ballpoint pen, he drew some circles at the base of my neck where the collarbones joined at the ribcage and took measurements with a small ruler.

"Feel this," he said softly, leading my fingers to the areas he'd just marked.

I recoiled in horror as my hands froze on the walnut-sized hard knobs that lay just behind the collarbones. My mind jumped wildly.

WHY HAVEN'T I FELT THESE BEFORE?

I'd showered each morning and sometimes had a bath after the sweats. Not once had I felt the lumps. I was shaken to the core.

Dr. Chritchley said, "the lymph nodes are extremely swollen in your neck and abdomen. I'm going to request a biopsy be done on one of them". He picked up the phone on the desk and made the arrangements. As he spoke, I tried to come to grips with what he had just told me.

Lymph nodes. Swollen. Biopsy.

How many times had I heard those words before. It had never meant anything to me in the past. This is the kind of thing that only happens to other people.

I slowly dressed. My head was spinning and I felt as if everything was moving in slow motion; as if I were in a surrealistic movie, where nothing really made sense. I stood there like a robot, my arms limply hanging at my sides.

When Dr. Chritchley hung up the phone, he stood, turned to me, grabbed both my shoulders in his outstretched arms and said in a strong, positive tone, "Wally, I want to make you healthy again so you can work hard and pay lots of taxes".

Humor in the cancer clinic. His remark broke the tension. The balloon of roiling emotion suddenly deflated, like it had been pricked by a pin. At the moment, it was the best medicine that could be prescribed.

But the joy was short-lived.

I asked him what the diagnosis was. He motioned for me to sit in the chair next to his desk and he sat down. The humor evaporated instantly. He looked at me directly in the eyes. I knew what he had to say would be something that would change the course of my life.

"If it is what I think it is, you have advanced Hodgkin's disease. I think you'll probably have to go through a minimum of six but more likely, eight months of chemotherapy and four weeks of radiotherapy".

My eyes glazed. *Did I hear right? Did he just say -six to eight MONTHS of chemotherapy?*

I felt myself reeling and grabbed the armrests of my chair. Dr. Chritchley realized my state and held my shoulders. He was grinning again. I reached out and grabbed the tops of his forearms, as if trying to extract some of his energy and positive vibes. I forced a weak grin.

"I'm going to stage you now – that is to find out how advanced the Hodgkin's is". He explained the process. First, there would be more blood tests, then the bone marrow extract and finally the lymphangiogram. I tried to take in what he was telling me but most of it didn't register. I felt as if I were standing in the middle of a Los Angeles freeway with cars and trucks blasting by me in both directions at a hundred miles an hour.

In the din of confusion, though, I did hear him say something about how *a couple* of them might be unpleasant.

He stood up and I followed him. We shook hands and he said I'd be getting a call shortly about the surgery to remove one of the lymph nodes in my neck. We would meet again to discuss the results of the biopsy and to schedule the remainder of the procedures.

In spite of the roller coaster ride of emotions and uncertainty I'd just experienced, I also felt a bit of the calmness like I did at that pivotal first phone call from oncology. I knew I could put my life and trust into the hands of Dr. Chritchley. He'd given me some statistics during the examination. Patients with Hodgkin's had a slightly higher chance of survival compared with other forms of cancer. He said a 70 percent survival rate was not uncommon. As well, knowing what I was facing gave me something concrete to deal with.

I left the hospital and quickly walked to my car in the parking lot. I looked at my watch. It was 4:40. Twilight had descended in the Okanagan as the sun set behind the mountains to the west. I zipped my jacket up to my chin to keep out the cool February breeze. As my left hand touched my neck, I again thought of the enlarged lymph node.

Gingerly and with trepidation, I touched the hard object just under the collar of my jacket. A shiver shot up my spine and then I suddenly got angry. I wanted to reach in and tear out the offending lymph nodes. I'd learned they were connected throughout the body. I envisioned pulling them out and hurling them to the ground. Writhing in their death throes, I saw myself stomping on them in rage. I jumped on them until they were ground into the earth, to be scattered like dust in a storm.

A violent shiver racked my body and I was sweating again. I had difficulty unlocking my car door. I dropped into the seat, closed my eyes, grabbed the steering wheel and placed my forehead on it. The scene I'd just envisioned made me limp.

Another chilling question struck me – one I should have asked earlier.

What about the other 30 percent?

The reality hit me head-on. I had two choices.

I could live – or die.

In the solitude of my car, I shook my head at the second option. I vowed I would do everything humanly possible to live. I knew I'd have to lean on my faith, family and friends to help me get through whatever lay ahead of me.

I uttered a silent prayer.

God, please give me strength. I didn't make any deals. I simply asked God to give me the wherewithal to make it through the uncertainty over the upcoming months, day by day. *If you give me strength each day, for whatever I'm faced with, I will accept the rest of the responsibility to live – for my family.*

I jolted upright, my hands wracked with pain. I looked at them and realized I had a death-grip on the steering wheel. Slowly, I relaxed and released my fingers, which had turned white. I started the car and drove back to the duplex.

Caroline had supper ready and as we sat down to eat, I recounted the examination with Dr. Chritchley. I looked at Jodi and Chris, then Caroline and told them I had advanced Hodgkin's disease.

Silence fell on our table. I showed each one the swollen lymph nodes which were visible at close range. I saw the concerned looks. I tried to be upbeat and told them what Dr. Chritchley had said about paying taxes after getting better and the statistics he'd given me. They didn't laugh.

We finished supper, cleaned up and the kids disappeared to do their homework.

A half hour later I was watching TV and Caroline was in the laundry room. I looked up when Jodi slowly approached me. I could read utter confusion and pain in her young eyes. She stopped right in front of me. In a soft, halting voice with an edge to it, she asked something which I was totally unprepared for.

"Daddy, are you going to die?"

Her words struck me full force, like a knife embedding itself directly into my chest. I couldn't bear the thought of knowing my family might spend the rest of their lives without me.

She would get her driver's license and I wouldn't enjoy the moment when she'd wheel away, by herself for the first time. Her twelfth grade graduation, where she'd be accepting her diploma without her dad; making plans for university – *and didn't every dad have the right to give his daughter away at her wedding?*

I remembered holding Jodi moments after she was born. *Was I being selfish?*
Yes!

She'd heard the statistics at supper. I again told her of the percentages and that Hodgkin's patients had a good chance of survival. She didn't care about that. Again with her lips quivering in anguish and shaking with emotion, she asked, "daddy are you doing to die?"

There was only one answer I could give my precious 15 year old daughter. I gently took her hand and softly pulled her onto my lap. I held her close, wrapped my arms around her and tucked her head under my chin. I softly whispered the answer she needed to hear.

"No, pumpkin, I'm not going to die".

I pulled up her face and gave her a kiss on the cheek. She lowered her head again. She put her arms around my neck and we sat there holding each other. My eyes stung as they filled with tears that slowly rolled down my cheeks onto the top of her head. After several minutes, we stood up together and I gave her another peck on the cheek and smiled to give her reassurance. She returned to her room to finish her homework.

I stood transfixed. I was barely aware of the muted sounds coming from the TV.

The moment I'd uttered those words, I'd made a pact with not only her, but with Chris and Caroline – and myself. *I have to live; for all of us.*

Other than the times of the deaths of my parents, there wasn't another moment in my life where I'd felt so abjectly helpless, so spent and in need of so many answers.

Through the din of this ever-maddening, mental upheaval, I choked back more tears. It was the only time I can ever remember questioning what was happening. In my mind's eye, I stretched out my arms, clenched my fists and screamed out in rage and despair.

God – this isn't fair! WHAT HAVE I DONE TO DESERVE THIS!

The split second that blasphemous reaction to my child's innocent question left my brain, I knew the answer. I did not – could not blame God. I knew the Creator was not responsible for the disease. But I was absolutely convinced God would be with me as I traveled through the valley of the shadow of death, through the unknown, to be with me on a journey that would forever change me in whatever time I had left on this earth.

I again prayed for strength. Strength to make it through one day at a time.

Suddenly, I couldn't stand anymore. My legs had turned to jelly and like removing the plug in a bathtub full of water, I felt my energy swirl and ebb away. I stumbled into our bedroom, my eyes brimming and threw myself facedown on the bed. I buried my face in my pillow, my body wracked with sobs.

Chapter 4

THE FOLLOWING FOUR WEEKS flew by in a blur of medical diagnostic activity.

Dr. Chritchley had requisitioned me to meet with Dr. Keith McIvor at his downtown office the following afternoon. He was the surgeon who would remove the enlarged lymph node in my neck. An hour before the appointment, I went to Penticton Regional Hospital for a series of chest X-rays that Jack had ordered. He told me it was standard protocol to see if there were any growths or tumors present in that area. When the pictures were done, I drove to Dr. McIvor's office.

Keith was a tall man with a rugged appearance. It looked like he spent a lot of time outdoors. He invited me to sit down as he read the transcript from my cancer specialist.

"Hodgkin's, huh?" he said looking up over his glasses after reading the first few lines. "How are you feeling?"

"As best as I can under the circumstances, I guess. I'm trying to stay positive", I replied. "Let me feel your neck", he said. He reached across the corner of the desk and gently kneaded the hard knobs behind my collarbones for a moment. As with Dr. Chritchley, I felt comfortable and at ease with Dr. McIvor.

"Boy, they're pretty big", he responded. I nodded with a sinking feeling. He reached for his phone and made the arrangements. "I've scheduled your operation for next Monday. It's day surgery so you'll be home by evening." He said he'd remove the lump on the left side of my neck and it would be quickly analyzed.

"Anything else?" I queried

"No". He paused, then said, "try to relax. We have some very good medical people in town". He handed me an envelope and added, "give these to the receptionist at the hospital when you check in". I shook his hand and thanked him.

The following Monday, Caroline drove me to the hospital along a route that was becoming all too familiar. We didn't say much and I knew she was as nervous as I was. After handing over the envelope at the admitting station, she kissed me goodbye and said she'd be back to take me home after the procedure. I was ushered into the surgical ward. I changed into the hospital gown and soon I was lying on a stretcher, ready to be wheeled into the operating room. After answering a few more questions from a nurse, I was prepared for the surgery and moved into the corridor.

"We meet again".

I recognized Keith McIvor's voice. I looked backward up to the ceiling and saw him as he approached my gurney from behind. He walked up to my right and we shook hands again. He was smiling.

"This won't take long and I promise I'll do a neat job of sewing you up again".

He and I exchanged wisecracks as I was wheeled into the O.R. I was introduced to the other members of the team and after the I.V. had been inserted into the back of my right hand the anesthetist said "count backward from ten". I made it to seven when everything went black.

The biopsy proved the lymph node was malignant as Dr. Chritchley suspected.

I had Hodgkin's disease. Lymphoma. Cancer.

Even though we'd suspected the worst, the final positive diagnosis still came as a shock. Like the sound of a bell signaling the start of a championship bout, the fight of my life had begun. *Will I come out of my corner swinging like a fiend? Or take a defensive posture and keep my gloves up to ward off the sinister blows, hoping I wouldn't suffer a fatal, knockout punch.*

I didn't have a choice. I knew I would have to charge out of my corner, snarling and wailing away with everything I had, to summon every ounce of strength within me to defend myself.

It was time for the Hodgkin's-specific medical testing to begin. I endured blood work, provided urine samples and was poked, prodded and pricked. Dr. Chritchley also ordered a second set of chest X-rays. He told me there was something that made him uneasy in the first set of pictures. I told myself *if I spend anymore time in X-ray my ribs will start to glow in the dark.*

Then came the bone marrow extraction, the first of two intensive, invasive procedures. It's a good thing I'd never heard of it. The pathologist was to take a sample of fluid from my pelvis which would be analyzed to determine if the cancer had spread to the marrow. If so, the prognosis would be more grim. I was apprehensive about the test.

Dr. Chritchley had given me a quick overview of the procedure and said it would be uncomfortable. The pathologist would use a device shaped like an ice pick with a long needle to draw the bone marrow.

"How long is it?" I asked.

"About six inches". I shuddered at the mental picture.

On the morning of the examination, I was ushered into a small rectangular, doorless room about six by ten feet in diameter. A narrow cot was attached to the wall on my right. To the left were several shelves on which sat some electronic equipment along with surgical tools that were wrapped in green cloth. I could see the tips of several of the instruments.

The assistant tried to put me at ease with small talk. At one point he asked if I wanted to see the device – the one that would be inserted in my hip. I nodded and he showed it to me and I could see the similarity between it and a small ice pick.

It had a sophisticated handle with a thin, hollow steel tube extending 90 degrees from the middle of the handle. The diameter of the tube was only about a sixteenth of an inch. The business end had a very sharp point which made me wince.

The pathologist arrived, a big man with a beard. His name was Harvey Speirs.

We shook hands and he explained what he was going to do. As he spoke, he unwrapped the bundle of instruments from the green cloth. He asked me to undo my belt and lay face down on the cot. Moments later, my jeans were at my knees and my shorts halfway down my butt. There is nothing that makes a person feel more vulnerable than lying on one's stomach with shirt up and shorts down while the doctor, standing beside you is putting on rubber gloves.

He told me he would first numb the area where he was going to insert the large tool. "It's impossible to freeze bone so when I get past the skin and tissue you are going to feel what I am going to do". The words made me grit my teeth.

I felt the jab on my skin on my right hip a couple of times and within moments the area was numb from the anesthetic. I was conscious of his fingers probing to see how much of the area was frozen.

I was facing him and saw him turn his back for a moment as he reached for *the* instrument. I became increasingly nervous.

I lifted my head, turned away and looked at the wall, only inches away from my nose. "Ready?" he asked.

"Uh-huh"

I clenched my fists and teeth. My body stiffened.

For a few seconds I didn't feel much pain. Then, a sudden, sharp twinge made me wince as he found the area of the pelvis he would enter. I grabbed a handful of cot in my fingers and squeezed. The pain rapidly intensified, biting with every millimeter the shaft entered the bone.

"This will hurt!" he quickly shot out, then pushed.

A moment later, in a searing flash, it felt like the entire length of my intestines was being drawn up into the tiny opening of the needle as the device sucked out the bone marrow.

The operation lasted only a few seconds. When he pulled it out, my body was stiff as a board, my muscles from head to toe as taught as the string on a hunting bow. I was sweating profusely and blinked hard to clear my eyes.

Then slowly, inch-by-inch, muscle-by-muscle, I unwound myself. I blew some of the perspiration from my mustache. I slumped down, fully spent, like a deflated balloon.

"That's it", Dr. Speirs said. He asked the assistant to cover the puncture point with a large piece of gauze and instructed me to lie still for ten minutes to allow any bleeding to stop. As he left, he told me Dr. Chritchley would see me within a day or so to discuss the lab results of the bone marrow biopsy.

In short order, the gauze was removed and a small bandage applied to my butt. I pulled up my shorts and the assistant helped me with my jeans. I sat up and gingerly swung my legs over the side of the cot and stood up. I tucked in my shirt and walked slowly to the parking lot.

I felt like I'd been spanked – hard. When I got to my car and opened the door, I had to hold onto the side of the roof with both hands and slowly lower myself into the driver's seat. I instinctively took the pressure off my right cheek by putting all my weight on my left buttock.

I leaned 15 degrees left, hard against the door as I drove home.

To get out, I reversed the process, using my arms to hoist myself up and out.

When I got into the house, I breathed a long sigh of relief. "I'm glad that one is over", I told Caroline when I got in the door. "The first major procedure is finished".

I had celebrated much too soon. There had been a communication breakdown.

The requisition for the bone marrow extract should have

read 'remove marrow from *both* sides of the pelvis'.

The following week I again found myself on my stomach with my butt exposed as Dr. Speirs was putting on his rubber gloves.

Chapter 5

A FEW DAYS LATER I was back at the lab, on my stomach, my pants down around my knees receiving another six inch intrusion on the other side of my pelvis.

The drive home was even more interesting because I hadn't fully recovered from the 'bite' of the first procedure. I felt every bump in the road on my beleaguered backside.

By that time, the team of medical specialists had begun to zero in on the stage of Hodgkin's. Thankfully the disease had not entered my bone marrow. Dr. Chritchley had given me the good news a couple of days after the second bone marrow extraction. There was one more major, definitive test, the Lymphangiogram. I'd never forgotten what Jack had told me the first time we met. Something about it *not being a very pleasant experience*.

The procedure was scheduled at 12:30 p.m., Tuesday March 15 at the Kelowna General Hospital. I had been instructed to remember two things by the receptionist who had called me two days earlier to set it up.

"Bring slippers and make sure you have a ride home".

Retired friends of ours, Doreen and David Stevenson drove me to the hospital that morning and in the one hour drive we discussed my situation. They wished me well when I was dropped off at the large sliding glass doors near the emergency entrance.

After checking in, I was led to a large, fairly stark room,

much like the one in which an X-ray machine might be situated. It was full of electronic devices that droned in low tones. The lights on the panels housing diagnostic equipment blinked while digital timers flashed numbers. A large examination table was stationed in the middle of the room. A nurse greeted me with a warm smile and said she'd be with me during the 4 1/2 hour process.

Four-and-half hours – what are they going to do? Take me apart?

I'd suspected the procedure might take some time when I'd spoken about it with Dr. Chritchley but I certainly did not expect it to take most of the afternoon.

She read the concern on my face and laughed. "Don't worry. It's a long process because of the time it takes for a specific liquid which must be administered into your body so the doctor can determine the stage of your Hodgkin's", she answered. "We'll fill you in with more details as we progress".

She asked me to relax and make myself comfortable. I sat on a chair near the examination table. I was dressed in a T-shirt, loose-fitting sweatpants and a sweatshirt.

Because the lymphangiogram was conducted on my feet I didn't have to wear a hospital gown. A second nurse had joined us and she detailed the procedure from beginning to end. I didn't like the part about needles between my toes.

I thought *it surely can't hurt as much as that harpoon into my butt*. She then asked me to lie on my back on the table. I didn't have slippers, so I wore an old pair of sneakers with the laces out. I dropped them on the floor next to me.

She removed my socks and rolled my sweatpants halfway up my shins. I was given a couple of pillows for my head which gave me a good view of my feet. A few minutes later the doctor walked in with another nurse, introduced himself and his assistant to me and took a seat on a stool near my feet.

He said he would inject a dark liquid into the webbing between my toes to make visible the tiny blood vessels just under the skin on the tops of my feet. They had to be identified so a hair-thin needle could be inserted into the microscopic veins in both feet.

A clear honey-colored dye was to be pumped slowly into my feet and the solution would wind its way through the entire lymphatic system in my body. An X-ray the following day would determine the stage of the Hodgkin's disease.

I'd been subjected to a variety of intrusive, sometimes painful examinations. The lymphangiogram was another one in my journey to the final diagnosis. The specialist had told me he couldn't freeze the soft tissue between the toes and that it would hurt.

What else in new?

He swabbed the areas between the toes on each foot and reached back for the device he would use to inject the first liquid. The instrument resembled a turkey baster with a syringe at the business end.

Holy smokes. Maybe I shouldn't be watching this.

"Ready?"

I got up on my elbows and heard Dr. Chritchley's voice, echoing in my head, *the lymphangiogram might be unpleasant.*

He placed the syringe between the first two toes on my right foot and gave a quick poke. A searing pain shot into my foot at the point of the injection. When he pushed the plunger to force the dark blue liquid into the webbing, the pain exploded.

As with the previous two examinations, my fists again were clenched into the sides of the material on the cot. The nurses, one on each side of me, held my shoulders firmly. They knew what my reaction was going to be.

My white-knuckle ride continued until he finished; three injections in each foot. It lasted only a few minutes but it felt as if the procedure would never end.

When he was done, I let my elbows go limp and I collapsed, completely drained. One of the nurses came over with a towel and wiped the sweat from my face and neck. The areas between my toes were on fire causing my feet and calves to twitch in discomfort. They throbbed with each heartbeat.

"Beats isometrics, doesn't it", I mumbled to the doctor. He smiled and said he'd be back in fifteen minutes. "By then the coloration of the veins will be complete".

The nurses did their best to comfort me and asked if there was anything I needed. I said I was hungry and was given a menu. The turkey sandwich and orange juice that I requested arrived a few minutes later and I ravenously devoured the small meal.

Just as I finished, the specialist returned to complete the second stage of the lymphangiogram. He took my blood pressure and pulse and told me they were fine.

With a syringe, he froze the tops of both feet about halfway from the toes to the ankles. After a couple of minutes he tested them with a sharp instrument. They were numb.

"Do you want to see this part?" he asked.

"Is it going to hurt?"

"No"

I got up on my shaky elbows again and nodded. He took a scalpel and in morbid fascination I watched him cut a one-inch incision parallel with my feet. I was surprised at the lack of bleeding. Only a tiny amount of blood collected at the bottom of the cut. It was a very strange sensation to see him slice into my feet and have me feel absolutely nothing.

Through the incisions, he painstakingly searched for the tiny veins filled with the dark colored liquid. Near him on a cart was a small black machine, the size of a toaster that contained two vials, each filled with the honey colored liquid.

When he found what he was looking for, he expertly inserted into each incision, a very thin needle seemingly no thicker in diameter than a human hair. He attached a tiny rubber hose from each of the needles into the machine containing the liquid. I was attached and ready for the injections. He pushed a switch on the device and it began to hum. One of the nurses placed a sterile cloth over each incision.

I looked at the clock over the door. 3:05 p.m. The doctor had finished most of his work. He said the vials would be empty in an hour and he'd come back to suture the incisions. He left and I laid back down again, folding my hands across my stomach. I closed my eyes and tried to take my thoughts elsewhere, anywhere but the mundane surroundings of the hospital room.

My mind floated back to the spring of 1980 when I began the restoration of my antique 1962 Chevy hardtop. It was green and ugly when I dragged it home on a borrowed trailer. The front end had been hit, the windshield was cracked and the engine seized. I had the ability to envision it in all its former glory. Instead of a beat up, rusted hulk, I visualized an awesome thundering street machine. Caroline shook her head in disgust, muttering something like *when are you going to grow up and quit playing with old cars.*

I removed the worn-out 283 engine and automatic transmission, lifted the body off the frame and bit-by-bit and piece-by-piece, I disassembled the car and tagged every nut, bolt and fastener.

In reverse order, I put the car back together over a year. Finally, with a big grin on my face, I fired up the rebuilt 409 race engine that I'd purchased from a fellow in California. I'd installed a four speed transmission with a floor shifter. I grabbed the stick, hammered the accelerator and launched the Chevy. I released the clutch and listened with glee as the rear wheels screamed and laid two black strips of rubber in front of our house.

I shifted into second and the car shuddered and fish-tailed. More rubber. Then into third with the tires still smoking. Suddenly, I'd run out of street.

To slow down the ancient muscle car, I had to stand on the

brakes to decelerate 3,600 pounds of steel, engine and tires. I remembered the absolute exhilaration of driving the car. Man and machine, four speed and clutch, the massive engine just waiting to be unwound, just like in the Beach Boys' song. The dust, smell and sound of burning rubber was still with me at that moment, as if it happened only days earlier.

My daydream then drifted to the final addition I'd added to our house only months before we moved. I put a hammer and saw in my hand and built the deck behind our home.

Finally, I thought about all the exotic places Caroline and I would like to visit when our nightmare was over. I tried to imagine what Hawaii and Aruba might be like.

Friends of ours who'd been there made the vacations sound magical.

My thoughts continued to flit around from family activities to playing hockey.

I felt a soft tug on my shoulder as one of the nurses woke me and said it was over.

I opened my eyes and squinted, trying to orient myself. The hum of the equipment reverberated in my ears again. The fluorescent lights directly above me caused me to shade my eyes with my hand until they adjusted to the brightness.

I looked down to see the other nurse slowly retract the needles from my feet and I felt a twinge as they were removed. A few moments later the doctor arrived to close the incisions. He froze again, the areas on top of my feet and ten minutes later, he'd closed up the last suture. He asked one of the nurses to bandage my feet, wished me well and we shook hands good-bye.

It was 4:25 when I sat up. With considerable effort, I swung my legs over the side of the cot. They felt like Jell-O. I slowly put my weight on my bandaged feet and struggled to get them into my lace-less sneakers. The tongues were pulled forward, allowing a lot of room.

I thanked each of the nurses for all they had done and

slowly shuffled to the pay phone in the lobby. I called Paul Willis, a long-time friend who had earlier in the week agreed to take me back home to Penticton. Caroline and I had known him and his wife Barb for 25 years. Paul's a big, bearded guy and an avid hunter and fisherman. We remained in Alberta while he and Barb had moved to British Columbia in 1972.

Paul was an usher at our wedding that year and we'd kept in touch over the decades. Through the years, we'd tried to visit each other as much as possible. When we moved to the Okanagan, we were also reunited with another old friend, John Arstall. The three of us had worked together at Western Grocers in Calgary in the late 60's and had formed a life-long bond.

Ten minutes later, Paul arrived at the front doors. I grunted as I gingerly hoisted myself up into his 4-wheel drive pickup. Because of my weakened state, the truck felt like it was three feet off the ground. He swung out of the hospital parking lot and headed south for the drive to Penticton.

Paul's great sense of humor lightened up the situation. As we wound our way through the city and onto the mile-long floating bridge which would take us to the west side of Okanagan Lake, I felt another sweat coming on. He told me I looked very pale.

"You want me to stop so you can puke?" he asked.

I looked at him and started to laugh. The way he said it struck me as being very humorous. "No, but you can turn up the heater", I replied as I popped two more Tylenol.

About ten minutes south of Kelowna, in Westbank, I felt better as I warmed up.

My sense of humor returned. I didn't realize how important it would be in my crusade to survive. I appreciated Paul's funny stories and jokes. We laughed the rest of the way home as dusk enveloped the valley. It was dark as we pulled up outside our house about 6 o'clock. Paul joined us for supper and he left for home about two hours later.

Caroline and I watched TV for a while and went to bed

about 10. In the dark silence we lay holding each other, each engrossed in our own thoughts, waiting for sleep. Even though my body was exhausted and sore, my mind was still racing. Rocketing ahead at full speed, without brakes and hurtling onto a track with no finish line in sight, I faced an unknown future; a movie without a finish.

I wondered how much of the ending was in my control.

As I waited for another night sweat, one hard fact again surfaced in my head.

Physically, mentally and spiritually, I was in for the fight of my life where the opponent was unseen and unheard and eating away at the very source of life, the cells in my body.

Chapter 6

CANCER IN ITS SIMPLISTIC definition is: an uncontrolled growth of cells in one's body. Hodgkin's disease is a lymphoma; cancer of the lymphatic system. The cancer is spread throughout the body via the blood and lymph (a clear fluid).

Of all cancers diagnosed yearly, one percent is Hodgkin's affecting about fifteen thousand Americans and one thousand Canadians.

The prognosis for successful treatment has been rising over the past several decades. Those with Non-Hodgkin's lymphoma (the disease Jackie Kennedy-Onassis had in early 1994) have a 50-50 chance of survival. She passed away in March of that year. I followed her final weeks with vested interest. I had studied both types of cancer and was saddened but not surprised when she died.

Hodgkin's usually strikes two primary age groups: those in their mid-teens to the age of 34; and people in middle age, usually 45 to 55. I fell into the second group.

Mario Lemieux is Canada's most famous Hodgkin's survivor. He was 29 when diagnosed.

There are three lymph node areas in the body: the neck, chest and abdomen. Each have a left and right side. The illness can affect the area above or below the diaphragm, or both.

In the previous chapters I mentioned I had to be 'staged'.

There are four stages of Hodgkin's with an "A" or "B" to each stage. They are:

> Stage one: only one lymph node area is involved.

> Stage two: two or more lymph node areas are involved on the same side of the diaphragm

> Stage three: two or more lymph node areas are involved on different sides of the diaphragm but no vital organs are affected

> Stage four: vital organs such as bone marrow, lung, liver and brain are involved.

I've tried to simplify this as much as possible. However, it really does not do justice to relegate Hodgkin's to such a one-dimensional view, but for ease of understanding, it's the best way of describing it.

If the cancer had spread to my bone marrow, it would've completely changed the protocol and prognosis.

I still often asked myself *what if I'd gone to a doctor sooner?*

But I knew I could not live with *'what if's'* and had to face reality.

I met with Dr. Chritchley the day after the lymphangiogram. In my old sneakers, I shuffled into his examination room and sat down. I was very nervous, my mouth dry and I had difficulty swallowing. I knew the staging would be quite high, given what I'd learned about the disease over the previous month.

Dr. Chritchley walked in a few minutes later and sat down across from me at his desk. He said 'hi' and flipped through some papers on his clipboard. He seemed on edge and had a concerned look on his face, which was unusual. I fought back panic and scanned his demeanor for more clues. He glanced at his notes again, put down his clipboard and stared me squarely in the eyes.

"Wally, we've got a real fight on our hands".

My heart stopped. The fear began to well up in my stomach. I struggled to maintain my composure.

"A couple of days ago, I got the results of the second set of chest X-rays," he added. He paused for a moment and said in a solemn tone, "They along with the lymphangiogram revealed that in addition to the cancer having invaded your lymphatic system and some of your internal organs, you also have two tennis ball-sized tumors in your chest cavity, one behind each lung."

He stopped for a moment and said, "Without treatment there's little chance for your survival".

The silence was deafening as I let that last statement sink in. "What's the verdict?" I asked in a hushed tone, barely able to get the words out.

"You've been staged at 3-B Hodgkin's".

3-B! I wasn't far from hitting the wall.

Chapter 7

Journal entry: Thursday March 24, 1994.

*The first day of the rest of my life. Today
I get my first chemotherapy treatment.
Chemotherapy. I can't get it out my mind. I'm
going to be injected with chemicals. Never in a
million years did I ever think I'd be facing this
treatment with drugs that can kill. Not only
bad cells but good ones too. However, I heard
something by an author with cancer interviewed
by Peter Gzowski on Morningside today. She
said 'chemotherapy' is a good word; a soothing
word. Because right in the middle is one of the
most comforting of all words: MOTHER.*

OTHER THAN THE TIME I was born, my wedding and the birth of my children, no other date in my life was as important as that day.

I began the first of sixteen chemotherapy treatments over eight months. The staging was finished, as were the myriad of tests, procedures, blood-letting, stitches and pain. I'd met with Jack Chritchley the day before I began the treatments. He told me the usual protocol for advanced Hodgkin's was at least eight months of chemotherapy and four weeks of radiation.

I walked into the hospital at 3:30 p.m., March 24th with my

wife, daughter and son, the loved ones who mattered most to me. Never before had I appreciated them as I did at that moment. I needed all the emotional and physical support possible. I knew my family would be my rock.

Close friends at my side would be another refuge in the calamity we were facing.

We were in their prayers and thoughts locally and hundreds of miles away. I held Caroline and Jodi's hands while Chris walked close beside us. He was like me, not one to show much emotion, his hands in his pockets. He tried to appear calm, but I knew how he felt. His heart was intertwined with mine. Both Caroline and Jodi were much more emotional. They had tears in their eyes. I was nervous, realizing I would be injected with lethal drugs. At the same time, though, I had to try to think of the chemotherapy as a life-saver.

We walked into the oncology waiting room. After briefly chatting with Pat we sat down. A short while later Christine Ransom, one of the oncology nurses popped through the door of the room and said in a cheerful voice, "come in". We'd met her a couple of times earlier and told us she would give the first chemo treatment to me.

She was a bubbly, upbeat medical oncology professional with a long history in cancer care and delivery of treatment.

We entered the main clinic, a large room about 12 by 30 feet in size. It was furnished with a half-dozen rocker recliners. In the middle stood a kitchen-type island about eight feet long. Placed on it was a row of binders in wire racks, color coded for each patient. One had my name on it.

Christine told us they kept meticulous records; noting every 'poke' and pill that was administered because each patient had a specific protocol.

I introduced Christine to each member of my family and the sense of trust came over me again as it had with Drs. Harries and Chritchley and with Claire. We had to believe the doctors, nurses, technicians and machines would make a difference.

Christine led me to a chair to the right of the room near a window. Outside, I could see the other wings of the hospital. Across the valley to the west, the mountains shimmered in the warmth of the early Okanagan spring. I sat down and was ready to be pumped with Oncovin, Procarbazine, Vincristine and the rest of the chemotherapy drugs that would prove to be as sinister as their names suggested.

We chatted constantly, mostly about the chemicals we'd heard about and that I'd be injected with. Christine inserted a needle in the back of my right forearm. To it, she attached a long, thin clear tube containing a saline drip from the plastic bag hanging from the intravenous pole on my right.

I watched the colorless liquid drip slowly. Drop by drop it left the pouch and began to fill a solid plastic tube about two inches long and an inch in diameter that was attached to the bottom of the it. She gave me several pills to help alleviate any possible nausea. "These are Maxaran, Stemetil and Ativan. You'll be given them about 15 minutes before each treatment".

She picked up her clipboard and gave us copies of the information describing the purpose of each drug in detail and the potential side effects. As she read aloud from hers she highlighted each one. Caroline's eyes slowly filled with tears as we silently followed along.

> VINCRISTINE – used to treat many kinds of cancer. Nausea and vomiting occur rarely. Hair loss may occur when receiving this drug, both on your head and body. Your scalp may become tender. Vincristine may have some effect on your nervous system causing changes in your muscle tone and action. You may notice a tingling or numbness in your fingertips. You may have difficulty in buttoning your shirt, holding a pen or picking up small objects. Difficulty walking or climbing stairs

should be reported.

PROCARBAZINE – is a drug used to treat mainly Hodgkin's disease. It is a capsule that is taken by mouth. Nausea and vomiting may occur, especially in the first few days of treatment. The doctor may give you a prescription for an anti-nausea medication. Procarbazine may have some effect on your nervous system such as tingling or weakness in hands and feet and unsteadiness in walking. Also muscle aches and pains. You may experience insomnia, nightmares and mood changes. Foods like aged cheese, yogurt, yeast extract and red wine may interact with this drug.

VINBLASTINE – a drug which is used to treat many kinds of cancer. It is injected. Most patients experience little or no nausea. White blood cells (which fight infection) may be decreased 4 – 9 days after treatment. Hair loss may occur on both head and body. Total baldness is possible. Injection sites may become sore and tender. Warm compresses may offer some relief.

BLEOMYCIN – this is also an anti-cancer drug which is injected into a vein. Some people may develop fever and chills a few hours after treatment. Do not scratch your skin while receiving this drug. Hair loss may occur within several weeks after the first treatment. Sore mouth may occur after a week of treatment. Teeth should be brushed with a soft toothbrush. Some people prefer a Waterpik to keep teeth and gums clean. Sore mouth may be soothed by baking soda mouthwashes 6 times daily. Commercial mouthwashes are not recommended because the alcohol further irritates the mouth. Avoid hot, spicy foods and acidic fruit drinks. A soft consistency, non-irritating diet can help make eating easier. Bleomycin can cause skin reaction of some type, like skin rashes, increased color or darkening of the skin over some areas, or thickness of the skin in palms and fingers. Your doctor may order tests to check this. Treatment to Bleomycin will make you sensitive to oxygen. Uncontrolled oxygen should be avoided except in an emergency and you should avoid increased oxygen pressure as in scuba diving. <u>The duration of risk after chemotherapy is unknown</u>. Inform new doctors, dentists or anesthetists that you have been treated with Bleomycin before you receive any surgery.

DOXORUBICIN – a drug used to treat many kinds of Cancer. It is a clear red solution that is injected. Nausea and vomiting may occur 3 – 4 hours after treatment and may last for 12 hours. An anti-nausea injection may be given when you receive your chemotherapy. Doxorubicin can cause burning if it leaks onto the skin surrounding the injection site. White blood cells and platelets (they help blood clot) may be decreased 6 – 13 days after treatment. Regular blood tests are done to monitor your blood counts. Hair loss is common, both with head and body. Sore mouth may occur a week after treatment.

CYCLOPHOSPHAMIDE – a drug used to treat many kinds of cancer. Nausea and vomiting may occur six or more hours after treatment. The doctor may give you a prescription for anti-nausea medication. Cyclophosphamide can irritate your bladder. To minimize this, it is important to drink 2 – 3 liters of fluid before, day of and day after treatment. It is important to empty your bladder frequently. A stuffy, sneezy feeling in your nose may occur 10 – 30 minutes after your injection. White blood cells may be decreased 8 – 15 days after the injection. Regular blood tests will be taken. Hair loss is common and may involve all of your hair. Notify your doctor if any of the following occur: signs or symptoms of an infection such as fever, cold symptoms, cough, pain or swelling of any areas of the body, ulceration or abscess (pus) forming anywhere on the body; easy bleeding or bruising; shortness of breath, difficulty breathing or hacking cough; blood in the urine – uncontrolled nausea, vomiting or diarrhea; redness, inflamation, pain or failure to heal at the injection site.

PREDNIZONE – a commonly prescribed steroid to help maintain weight.

Christine concluded, "you'll be on a 28 day cycle. That means we inject you now and again seven days from today. You'll then get three weeks off. That will give your body a chance to recuperate. Then we'll repeat the procedure again…" she paused momentarily, "…over eight months".

"Twenty-eight day cycle", I repeated. "just like having a period".

They laughed.

Caroline and I again scanned the sheets of paper. We'd just been bombarded with a blitzkrieg of information. It was almost impossible to comprehend and there was one compelling thought that didn't go away. The strong probability of hair loss was almost guaranteed.

I tried to imagine what I'd look like without hair. I thought of Telly Savalas, Yul Brenner and other actors who'd shaved their heads. Several questions bobbed to the surface.

Would my nose look too big? And what about my ears?

"Anymore questions?" Christine piped up with her bright smile. She looked at the four of us. We shook our heads.

"Okay, here goes" she said, picking up a syringe containing a clear, red liquid.

"This is the Doxorubicin. It will turn your urine the same color", she grinned.

"Wonderful", I said wryly. "Technicolor pee".

There were four small, round blue-tipped injection points on the long tube leading from the bottom of the I.V. bag. Christine swabbed the top one with alcohol. She placed the sharp tip of the syringe into the thin rubber membrane and gave a quick thrust and ever so slowly, pushed the plunger.

I watched in fascination as the red drug surged down the clear plastic tube. It became somewhat diluted as it neared the back of my hand and disappeared into the needle taped there.

The first chemotherapy drug had entered my bloodstream.

I felt the coolness of the liquid as it melted into my hand. I continued to stare at the point where it had entered. I felt no emotion. No fear.

No distress. No unpleasant thoughts.

Nothing.

I was surprised at my reaction. As I sat quietly, immersed deeply in my thoughts, I suddenly realized, however, the bell for round one had just been sounded in the fight of my life.

"Huh?"

Christine was tapping my shoulder. "How do you feel?"

I saw her withdraw the syringe. She had finished the first injection.

"Okay", I answered. Reaching behind me, she picked up the tray holding the drugs and gave me two small, white pills.

"Take these. They are also part of your regime".

"What are they?"

"They are the Prednezone pills, the steroids".

"Will they make me look like Arnold Schwartzenegger?" I chuckled out loud.

"No, not likely", she replied. "They will however, help

gain and maintain your weight". She picked up a second smaller syringe filled with a clear liquid. She found another entry point in the tube and inserted the needle.

"This is the Vincristine".

Caroline and I instinctively looked at the instruction sheet again, scanning for the sentence which had impacted us the most. *Hair loss may occur.* Again, I tried to picture myself bald. I asked her how she felt about the possibility.

"I'll love you just as much", she smiled.

We joked more about my soon-to-be follicle shortcoming. I looked at the kids.

They weren't smiling so we dropped the subject.

It was approaching 4:30. Chris had to leave for his 5 o'clock shift at Safeway. He gave me a good-bye hug. As he left, my stomach suddenly flipped over. It felt unsettled and my face flushed. I mentioned it to Christine and she told me it was a normal reaction.

She finished the remaining injections over the following half hour.

I didn't feel well at all when I got up to leave. I was unsteady on my feet and my stomach was churning. I felt an acidy taste in the back of my throat. We slowly left the clinic and I gave the car keys to Caroline when we got to the parking lot. She and Jodi constantly asked if I was okay.

I fought back the urge to vomit. I couldn't eat supper when we got home. A few minutes later, I was circled around the toilet bowl, violently throwing up. When I felt as if there was nothing left in my stomach, I staggered back into our bedroom. Twenty minutes later, I was in the bathroom again. The dry heaves had begun.

I remembered back to my college days when I could be found occasionally wrapped around a toilet repeating the same process, but from a different kind of liquid, one which was ingested, not injected.

The following morning family and friends arrived to help

us move. We'd purchased a house just before the diagnosis. I wished we'd been a little more patient, but the deed had been done. It was too late to back out of the agreement. Caroline could hardly wait to get out of the 'warehouse', as she called our rented duplex. When we moved in we unpacked only what we needed, knowing we'd be there for just a few months. More than half of the unpacked boxes sat ceiling-high in the kitchen.

My brother and his family came from Salmon Arm to assist us. Paul, Barb and John traveled to Penticton from Kelowna to help in the move while James Robinson from the radio station also chipped in.

My stomach felt like it was entwined around my spine because of the constant choking need to vomit. I tried to help with the moving but soon fell by the wayside, too ill to do anything.

Caroline called the Stevenson's and asked if they could take me to their home, just a few minutes away. I hadn't felt that weak for many years. With much difficulty, I swallowed my pride. I had to leave my masculinity behind. I couldn't lift or push anything. I had never felt that vulnerable. As I lay on the couch at Doreen and David's place the feeling of helplessness was overwhelming. I felt like an invalid.

Journal entry: March 25. I can't believe how beat up I feel.

It seems like I've been on a week-long drunk. When was the last time I was this sick? I don't remember. How I want to be with my family and friends moving our stuff. How many hours or days will I feel like this? God please give me strength.

At the time I didn't realize how much in prayer I would be over the following eight months. As well, my skin would've

crawled if I had realized how much more damage the chemotherapy would do.

Chapter 8

*Journal entry: March 28. It's been four days
since my first 'poke'. I called in sick at work
today. I ate two poached eggs, the first time
since my chemo I've eaten solid food. I've put
away several bottles of ginger ale and Sprite,
however. My stomach is really sore from all the
vomiting. Caroline and the kids are constantly
trying to comfort me. I feel very uneasy. I feel
like I'm losing control. I'm getting scared.*

I FELT GUILTY NOT going to the station because I'd only been
employed for four months. It wasn't the way I had planned
for things to happen. Over the previous twenty years in
broadcasting, fourteen of which I did a morning radio show, I
missed only a handful of shifts because of illness. In the past I
often forced myself to go to work at 4:30 in the morning with
a cold or flu when I felt I should have remained in bed.

I stayed in my housecoat for most of the day, not doing
much. My body was in neutral but my mind was still in gear,
leading me in directions that frightened me. My thoughts
were rocketing a thousand miles an hour, in an explosion of
different emotions.

How am I going to work feeling this rotten?
When will I be able to keep food down?
How many of those awful side-effects we read about will affect me?

Will my hair fall out?
Will I make it?

The last thought haunted me, surfacing repeatedly. It was the most difficult to shake from my consciousness. It conjured up all the horror I could imagine. My spine chilled and I felt the blood drain from my face whenever the image blind-sided me.

Sweat formed on my brow and the numbing coldness, even in the warm spring sun was frightening.

In the mid morning I opened the sliding glass door to our small deck that faced the eastern mountains. I stepped into the blinding sunshine, causing me to squint and I sat in one of our deck chairs. Through the vacant lot across the alley behind our house, I watched the traffic on South Main Street as the cars and trucks criss-crossed in front of me. I wondered who the drivers were and where they were going. I saw trucks with signage of local businesses delivering fridges, living room sets, groceries or maybe tires.

Do they realize how fortunate they are…that they're not stuck on a patio somewhere fighting back nausea…not being able to work. Do they appreciate their good health?

For several moments I found myself getting angry. Then I realized I had to take everyone out of the equation. I could not wish, hope or plead away what I was facing. I looked over the last decade of my life and realized it was to myself I should be asking questions, not to anonymous drivers.

Did I enjoy and revel on my own good health?
Had I looked after myself properly?
Was there anything I could have done in the past to prevent myself from being where I was at this moment – fighting for my life?

Like the waves that crash to shore on a beach clouding the water with sand, there were no answers. I would never know for certain.

Occasionally an ambulance sped by, its siren screaming over the traffic noise.

Perhaps someone had fallen, been involved in a car accident or suddenly become ill.

Maybe a cancer patient who… I let the thought trail off.

The grass was greening and the trees were budding. The next door neighbor to the south had several cherry trees near our six foot fence. She'd told me we could pick the fruit from the branches that grew out over our property.

I tried to nap around mid-day but it was futile. Later I prepared supper, ate a couple of mouthfuls, and about 9 fell into bed, spent from a day riding on an emotional roller coaster.

I went back to work the following day, still queasy but feeling a bit better. I was finally able to eat regularly for the first time since my 'poke' although the portions were much smaller. I thought back to the times my friends teased me about my enormous appetite. "How come a little guy like you can eat like a horse and not gain any weight?"

The day after I returned to work coincided with my second treatment. Oncology protocol required me to meet with Jack Chritchley a couple of hours after getting the morning blood test prior to each treatment. He would then determine if I could get the chemo. The most prolific and important indicator was the 'white count'. If the number of white cells in the blood was too low, the injections and pills had to be suspended.

Many patients became very ill because of the treatments. While killing the cancer cells, the chemicals also destroy some of the white cells which are crucial in maintaining a healthy immune system. Patients are much more susceptible to even the slightest infections or colds.

I'd been warned by Claire to not shave with a razor. Cuts and scrapes were potentially life-threatening. She'd also instructed me to stay away from crowds to lessen the chance of contracting a communicable disease. Before my first poke, Dr. Harries had given me an injection to ward off pneumonia, one of the most deadly illnesses a chemotherapy patient could contract.

The answer was simple. *Maybe I should become a hermit.*

I shook my head to eliminate that stupid thought. I looked for my twenty year old Philishave that sounded more like an old gas lawnmower than an instrument to shave one's face.

At eight the following morning I was back at the hospital lab with a nurse who was coaxing up a large vein in my right arm for my bloodwork. Three hours later I was sitting in Jack's office.

"How are you feeling?" he asked, spiritedly.

He took notes as I detailed the intimacy I experienced with my toilet over three days the week before. He stopped his writing and looked up quickly. "Oh, I'll fix that".

He reached for his prescription pad, wrote on it and handed the piece of paper to me.

"Take this to your druggist, it'll make a world of difference – and you can stop your love affair with your toilet."

He'd ordered a pill called Ondansetron for combating nausea in cancer patients. It's also known as Zofran, which is what we called it. Just before he left, he referred to his clipboard and said, "your blood counts are okay so we can proceed with today's treatment." He took my blood pressure and pulse and asked me to check with Pat for the time when I would get the poke.

I walked back to reception and asked when I was to return.

"Drop in about 2 this afternoon," she replied. I looked at my watch and saw I had a couple of hours before the treatment so I drove home to have a light lunch. On the way I stopped at our drugstore and left the prescription for the Zofran.

The pharmacist took a look at it and told me she could have it ready in a few minutes and invited me to wait. I told her I'd come back.

"Ah…do you know how much they cost?" She asked after scanning the piece of paper a second time.

"No."

She paused a moment, then said, "eighteen dollars...*each*."

It's a good thing I wasn't eating or drinking anything at that moment because I'm sure I would've spouted like Shamu at Sea World. I asked her if I could speak to the pharmacy supervisor. I told her we'd have to make monthly payments on the pills. She said she was quite sure her manager would approve the arrangement and added, "don't worry, we've done this before".

I thanked her and said I'd be back in an hour. On my way back to the hospital, I returned to the drugstore to pick up my pills. The pharmacist handed me the container and I saw through the clear plastic behind the label that they were a golden hue. *Makes sense* I mused as I toyed with the vial. *At eighteen bucks a pop, gold is a fitting color.*

I arrived back at oncology just before 2 p.m. and took a seat. After 20 minutes Pat motioned me to speak with her. She said Dr. Chritchley was behind on his schedule.

"It's quite common," she said and explained that as new patients were diagnosed, he would spend as much time as needed with each person. I tried to imagine how emotionally draining it must have been for him to tell each patient of the struggle ahead with cancer.

I remembered how gentle he was in his conversation with me about my diagnosis.

He never once looked at his watch. Time was not an issue. I realized oncologists wear many hats. They have to be doctor, listener, psychologist, counselor, confidant and friend.

Pat suggested I go home. "Call me every half-hour," she instructed. That became a standard procedure for the remaining fourteen pokes. At four o'clock, she asked me to come in. The kids had just come home from school and Caroline was still at work. On the phone, she told me she felt guilty for not being able to be with me. I knew she wanted to be by my side again.

Christine set up the I.V. as I settled into a chair and looked around me. A half-dozen people were in various stages of treatment. A couple of women had scarves wrapped around their heads. One man wore a baseball cap. I didn't see any hair under it and tried not to stare. Again I visualized myself bald and shuddered.

We chatted as she handed me the pre-poke pills including the Zofran, which I'd given to her when I walked into the room. I gobbled them down and waited for the nausea to envelop me as the toxic chemicals spilled into my bloodstream.

I was in for a pleasant surprise. Even though my face flushed and got warm again, the flu-like symptoms that caused me to be ill the previous week did not surface. It was wonderful. I ate a small supper that evening and didn't get sick. I felt better over the following few days and was filled with new enthusiasm at work. I also began to dismantle the wooden sides of a deck on top of our carport. The previous owners had built a sun-tanning facility there. But because of neglect, the roof coating had become rotten and severely weathered allowing water to pour onto the concrete floor whenever it rained. I climbed the stairs each evening after supper with a crowbar and hammer in hand, determined to remove the covering. As the days passed, however, it became more and more difficult to walk up the fifteen steps to the roof as I tired quickly. My arms began to tremble if I exerted myself too much. Trying to pull four inch rusted nails proved to be difficult. My breathing became labored and I sweated easily. But I persisted.

It was as if I was trying to fool my brain into fooling my body.

Eventually, I finally had the rotted cover removed and I busied myself with plans and drawings for enclosing the entire structure and placing a peaked, shingled roof over it.

Then three weeks to the day after my first poke, the first of several chemo side effects reared it's ugly head.

Journal entry: April 18. My hair is starting to

fall out.

It suddenly came out in bunches when I was in the shower this morning. To see my hair falling out like this creates a feeling of surrealism and unbelievability.

I expected this to happen but now that it has, I'm not really prepared for it. It makes the chemo real. There's no denying the drugs are in my body. I feel faint, watching my hair silently swirl at my feet and then disappear into the drain. It feels as if my very life is ebbing away beneath my naked feet. I knew I would lose my hair. But it still doesn't seem real.

That moment in the shower, with my hair snaking it's way with the water down my face, neck, chest, abdomen, legs and feet, was another eternally stored in my memory banks. It seemed to happen in slow motion. Like a movie, slowed down, frame-by-frame, I stood transfixed and stared down my body. All we'd read about that afternoon almost a month ago, was manifesting itself. How we'd chuckled about my possible hair loss.

It wasn't funny anymore.

Journal entry: April 20. I felt pretty good the last couple of days – almost normal. My stomach has been upset since yesterday however. I think it's because I start my second chemo cycle tomorrow. I know what to expect so I believe I'll be able to react to the drugs in a better fashion. I'm hoping I'm able to stay free of the nausea.

I have to create a gate from the fence along the alley after my next chemo session. I'll

concentrate on getting rid of the back lawn so I
can prepare the area for a concrete pad.

I'd finished cleaning up the top of the carport and turned my attention to getting rid of the sod at the back of our property. I wanted to pour a twenty-foot square concrete pad beside the carport. We'd built a large double car garage at our house in Lethbridge which I greatly missed.

I still felt fairly well even though I knew I was becoming weaker. My stomach was acting up more than usual. Twenty-two years earlier I was diagnosed with a hiatus hernia, a medical condition where the stomach wall protrudes beyond the valve at the bottom of the esophagus. It often causes heartburn and gas.

I'd learned to live with the condition, but paid the painful price of immense gastric discomfort if I ate spicy foods like a loaded green pepper, onion and pepperoni pizza. I could rock the house with my gaseous eruptions.

I discovered the chemotherapy drugs intensified the symptoms of the hernia.

> *Journal entry: April 21. Day one; cycle two. I*
> *walked into the clinic and a couple of nurses*
> *noted how my hair was thinning. I told them I*
> *would get a buzz-cut on Friday.*
>
> *After my meeting with Jack, I sat down in my*
> *favorite chair in the chemo room and mentally*
> *prepared myself for poke three. Only thirteen*
> *more to go.*

My hair continued to fall out in clumps and the top of my head soon looked like a patchy mess. It was time to see the barber.

On Friday, I went to work fighting the flu-type symptom. And for the first time, I was becoming concerned about my job. The drugs were making me feel like a zombie at times.

I had difficulty focusing on my presentations when meeting business owners. In radio sales, concentration and listening skills are a huge asset. Sales managers do not have a sense of humor when you fall asleep or drip with perspiration during a meeting with a prospective client. As well, I wasn't sure if I should be driving right after each poke because of all the drugs.

I saw the writing on the wall and knew I could not work much longer. Even though the night sweats and chill were diminishing, I was being subjected to something debilitating. I feared I was becoming a spectator in life, forced to the sidelines.

I didn't realize that I would eventually be dependent on my family and friends to help me do the things I'd taken for granted all my life.

Chapter 9

ON FRIDAY MORNING APRIL 22 at 10 o'clock, I climbed into the barber's chair. I'd come to know the proprietor because his shop was only two doors down from CIGV. He also knew of my Hodgkin's. I asked him for a 'buzz' and sat down. He put the black plastic cover over me and snugged its collar around my neck. When he placed the electric clipper at the hairline above my eyes, I was looking squarely at myself in the big mirror facing me. I thought of the hundreds of times at dozens of barber shops during my life that I'd sat in a similar chair. Never had I ever imagined my hair would all come off some day on purpose.

"Ready?" he asked.

"Do it," I said firmly.

For some strange reason images of the black and white documentary of Elvis Presley getting his hair shaved when he was drafted into the U.S. Army in the late 50's filled my mind. I recalled the media attention he garnered. There were movie cameras all around him. I remembered his good natured comments as he answered questions from reporters.

I looked at myself again. I was glad the shop was empty.

The barber touched the flat tip of the clipper to my forehead at the hairline and turned it on. It hummed to life. In one gentle swoop, like a farmer would lay flat a row of alfalfa with a swather at harvest, he cut a path down the middle, to the back of my head, then down to the neck. In my peripheral vision I saw the hair cascade from the sides and spill down into the creases of the black cape. Mesmerized, I watched my locks float lazily to the floor.

This is like a bad dream, I told myself.

He touched the front of my scalp again and the next layer of hair fell. He continued until the right side of my head was bare. In minutes, the hair from the opposite side was lying on the floor. He stepped back and asked, "how's that?"

I didn't answer right away because I was staring at my head. I looked like a peach with ears. It was almost comical, a weird kind of funny. The corners of my mouth were twisted slightly upward. I didn't know what to think. I wondered what my family would say when they saw me.

I remembered as a kid when my dad came home after being fitted with false teeth. My sister and brothers and I tried not to laugh, but couldn't hold back our snickers. He told us in no uncertain terms it was not a laughing matter and his stern look told us he wasn't kidding.

Will my kids laugh?

"Pardon?" I asked, returning to reality.

"How's that?" he asked again.

"Okay, under the circumstances, I guess."

I reached into my pocket to pay for the haircut but he didn't accept the money.

Instead he shook my hand and wished me well. I walked next door to the radio station and asked Jean King, the receptionist what she thought of my new look.

"Hey, it's not bad at all," she said, smiling.

I couldn't stop rubbing my head. My scalp felt like day-old stubble on my chin. I spent the rest of the morning getting some good-natured ribbing from many of the staff. I picked up Caroline after work. The look on her face was quizzical as she got into the car.

She didn't know whether to laugh or cry. She gently touched my head and asked if I was okay. I told her I wasn't sure.

One thing was for certain. The drugs had manifested themselves by their presence in my bloodstream. My mind kept flashing back to the one line on the information sheets about the side effects of the chemicals that seemed to be common to most of them. HAIR LOSS MAY OCCUR.

No kidding.

As we drove home, I constantly peeked in the rearview mirror and it still seemed surreal. The kids came in as we were preparing supper. They both stopped in mid-stride when they saw the barber's handiwork. I wished I had a camera to capture their expressions.

"What happened to your hair?" Jodi finally blurted out. She and Chris both knew the hair loss was a distinct possibility but were still not prepared for the reality. Over supper we loosened up and began to laugh about the hair situation. Stuff like, "boy Dad, you'll save money on shampoo," and "you'll be ready for work five minutes earlier."

The humor felt good and it was nice to be able to laugh again. For just a little while, we let ourselves go. The evening remained on a high, fun-filled note.

I was determined to keep myself up-beat and as positive as possible. I knew it was also critical to stay physically active. I spent the following couple of weeks removing the sod from the back lawn. I then created an opening to our six foot high fence facing the alley by hinging an eight foot long portion of it, allowing me to load up the strips of grass onto the back of our pickup.

It was during that time that another side effect of the chemotherapy surfaced. The numbness, as Dr, Chritchley had predicted a couple of months earlier, began to slowly invade my fingertips and toes and it became increasing difficult to hold onto a hammer, shovel or crowbar.

I got frustrated whenever I worked hard. I gritted my teeth and cursed under my breath whenever I couldn't control my tools. My body jerked in spasms when I tried to pull something heavy. At times it was difficult to lift my shovel when it was full. I wished I could climb out of my disintegrating body and get back to what I used to be, strong, vibrant and well.

I took breaks and leaned on my shovel more often than I wanted to and sipped frequently from my water bottle. One Saturday afternoon, I paused, wiped my forehead with a towel and drank deeply. As I leaned on my shovel, I was taken away by a daydream and thought about the thousands of miles I put on my bike over the previous decade. I missed the wind whistling through my helmet and hair.

I also smelled the musty, sweaty dressing rooms in the dozens of rinks in which I'd played hockey. I felt the stick in my hands, the puck cradled in the curved blade as I streaked up the ice. Like Bobby Hull, I turned on the jets and my legs pumped like mad, the steel on my skates slicing into the glass-like surface. Over the blue line, at full speed, I zeroed in on the goaltender. After splitting the defensemen, I deked them out and tucked the puck into the upper corner of the cage, the netting bulging. Triumphantly, I raised my stick high into the air to celebrate the goal.

I must've looked pretty silly standing there in the soil with my shovel pointing to the clouds. Sheepishly, I quickly looked around to see if anyone was watching and dropped it to the ground. I felt myself blushing.

Journal entry: April 25. Started my second cycle last Thursday and am still feeling queasy. I suppose this is what will happen during chemo weeks. I didn't expect it to last quite this long, however. When I feel like this, all I can do is go along for the ride and try to eat as much as I can and get as much rest as possible. (9:30 pm) I'm finishing up my drawings of the carport which I'm turning into a garage and will take them to city hall for approval when they're done. I'm

*waiting for Chris to get home from work and am
listening to Roy Orbison on Jodi's Walkman.
It's amazing how after 30 years, his music still
soothes me. Whenever I'm in a contemplative
mood, no one for me is easier to listen to than
Roy Orbison.*

*Journal entry: April 26. Woke up today with a
very sore stomach. It's like my hiatus hernia is
on fire. I couldn't finish my coffee. I've never
had this kind of heartburn since I was diagnosed
with the condition 20 years ago. It even hurt
to drink water. I am quite concerned. I got an
appointment with Jeff Harries and he prescribed
a medicine called Zytotec which he said should
help ease the pain. He cautioned me it might
take a day or so before it began to work.*

I took the medication and went to bed that night without eating supper. Every time I swallowed, I felt a stab of
pain in the middle of my chest where the esophagus joins
the top of the stomach. Everything I tried to eat or drink,
hurt.

I woke up the next morning with the condition having
worsened. Close to panic, I phoned Dr. Harries again but
he was doing his hospital rounds. I hurried to oncology and
after a long wait, met with Jack. He examined me and reiterated that the drugs Jeff had prescribed would work but it
might take a bit longer. He also reminded me of the toxic nature of the chemotherapy and with a pre-existing condition
like a hiatus hernia, the drugs were wreaking havoc on the
valve at the bottom of the esophagus. He told me to 'hang
in there'.

I tried to eat supper again that night but was thwarted
because of the intense discomfort. The best I could do was
force down a piece of unbuttered bread and a couple of swal-

lows of milk and I faithfully took the medication.

By the third morning, I could eat a bit. It still hurt to swallow but not as much as it did the previous two days. Gradually, over the following couple of days the pain subsided and I began to feel much more normal.

Normal. *What's normal anymore*, I thought. I had reached a new plateau of experience and everything was relevant. I tried to remember what it felt like to live without being dictated by a regimen of pill-taking, blood work and sitting in waiting rooms and clinics.

'Different', had become normal and part of my everyday living. Pain and discomfort had become constant companions. I had difficulty remembering what good health was like since starting my chemotherapy. I longed for the times we'd sat down to a good dinner and not have to be concerned about starting a fire in the pit of my stomach. I had also been given a bland food diet by Claire Davidson. The only excitement on my food that I was allowed was to use salt and pepper sparingly.

Pizza is number one on my list of what I'm going to eat when I'm done with all of this nonsense I promised myself.

I was quite sore from all of the physical work I'd been doing as well. Before my stomach problem manifested itself, my goal had been to get the carport enclosed. In my mind's eye, I saw a nicely completed structure housing the antique Chevy.

That vision slowly evaporated like the morning mist on the mountain tops around us as the weakness became more pronounced. My hammer felt like a 16 pound sledge. Exhaustion was a regular part of my routine from simple activities like walking and climbing stairs. My muscles were slowly losing their battle to the chemotherapy drugs. Even though the Prednizone assisted in putting back about five pounds, it was deceiving because it was mostly water retention.

I became pudgy, soft and weak. I noticed too, that my face was changing along with my body. The person who looked back at me in the mirror each morning was morphing into someone I did not recognize.

Better living through drugs was certainly not applicable to me.

Wedding day in Calgary, April 1, 1972.

Interviewing the Great One, Wayne Gretzky in Lethbridge in 1982. He was a pleasure to work with.

Packing up and moving from Lethbridge after 17 years. It was a very emotional time. That's Corey Thibert looking back.

The old 72 Chev pickup that took us through many years and memories, especially the one Jodi and I had lunch in. I still have it today.

Having lunch with the kids in our 'warehouse', our rental home when we first moved to Penticton. Notice the unpacked boxes.

The day after I had my head shaved, three weeks after the first chemotherapy treatment.

Our first trip back to Lethbridge after our move. Virtually no hair or mustache. I'm probably day-dreaming about my 62 409 Bel Air.

This is the car I rebuilt from scratch. It is still one of my favorite rides.

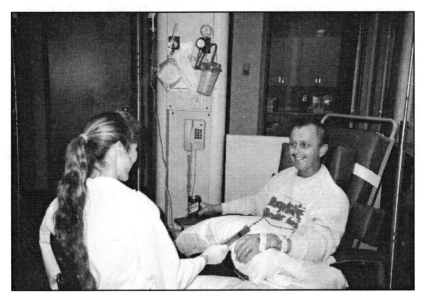

It's finally over! Getting my last chemo treatment from Tanis.
Notice what 8 months of chemotherapy does for one's complexion.

Back to normal with my family. I grew a beard because I could.

Chapter 10

Journal entry: April 27. Today was a pretty good day given that I'm between chemo sessions. My stomach still feels upset most of the time, although it's better. I weighed in at 150 pounds at the hospital during a routine checkup. I don't want to go any lower than that. Actually I want to get to 160 by the end of August. I'm eating as much as I can which really feels good, but sometimes I overeat and suffer from various degrees of indigestion. But in a week, I'll be feeling much better and hopefully I can start getting ready for the concrete to be poured for the pad. Most of the sod has been given away so I'll soon be ordering the gravel fill.

MY STOMACH CONTINUED ON it's wild, topsy-turvy ride. I was more susceptible to acid indigestion because of my hiatus hernia than most chemo patients who didn't suffer from the condition. During small talk with others going through treatment, I asked if they suffered from heartburn. Most told me they experienced some discomfort but nothing like I described. I often swallowed hard because my stomach felt like it was creeping up into the back of my throat. The uncomfortable, gagging sensation stayed with me for three or four days after each poke.

Another annoying result of the chemotherapy which was prophesized by the information given to us by Christine, was the metallic after-taste. It was so debilitating, even water and milk tasted terrible. It was as if cold, liquid aluminum had been poured over my teeth, gums, tongue and roof of my mouth. I was trying to drink at least six glasses of fluid a day but the metal-mouth sensation made just about everything taste horrible. I had to forgo the cream and two sugars in my coffee and drink it black.

Milk, which was one of my favorite beverages, was difficult to drink because of the acid tinge. I'd mentioned the condition to Jack and he said that was another side effect I had to deal with. With two growing teenagers in the house we consumed eight to twelve liters of skim milk a week. I bought some Lactaid which another patient suggested I should try. It neutralizes the lactose from milk for those who's stomachs cannot tolerate the enzyme. It didn't help me however and I concluded it was the chemicals that caused the burning sensation.

I'd been consuming protein drinks which were supplied free to me from the clinic. They were donated by the Canadian Cancer Society to help patients maintain weight. Each tin contained 350 calories and I usually drank two a day. When my stomach was able to tolerate it, I blended in a couple of scoops of ice cream which increased the caloric intake. As delicious as they were, the metal effect made them hard to ingest.

Journal entry: April 28. I finished my second cycle today. Only six more to go which means the treatments should end sometime near the end of October. They tell me I'll have to go to Vancouver for radiation therapy, which will probably go till Christmas. Anyway, I'm glad this one is over because the second session in each cycle drags me down more than the first. I feel lethargic. By tomorrow I hope to

be feeling better. On the bright side, I have a
couple of weeks in which I should be feeling
fairly normal. Yeah, right, Normal. I haven't
succumbed to feelings of depression yet. Claire
told me that many cancer patients go through
the dark days and some are affected much more
deeply than others. Even with the positive vibes
I get from everyone at the clinic, there's always
the possibility this might not work. Nobody
knows. It's imperative that I look after myself,
physically. I have to be much more conscious of
what I eat. Also when the treatments are over,
I'm going to have to work out religiously to get
back into shape again so that my lymph and
immune systems get back to normal once more.
There's that word 'normal' again.

In the dark, unlit, dangerous crevices deep in the back of my mind, I often fought to suppress the possibility of facing my death. Like a smelly, twisted weed that chokes off flowers, it festered. It took all my positive energy each day to keep the negativity from taking over. I thought how things might have been different had I chosen another life path. I'd visited the University of Calgary in the spring of 1969 and met with a counsellor in the Faculty of Education but I never followed it up. Jobs were plentiful in the late 60's so I went to work instead of earning a Phys Ed degree.

By now I'd be near retirement I thought. *I would have banked almost 30 years in education into a comfortable lifestyle with a good pension*

Instead, I was 47 years old, dangerously ill, unable to work with no benefits.

Journal entry: April 29. Today was an
exceptionally tough day. I stayed in bed till past
noon, making up for the sleeplessness of the past

couple of nights. I felt tired for most of the day.
My mouth really feels metallic, like Claire said it
might be. Days like today will simply have to be
write-offs. On a scale of 10, today is a 2.

By accident one afternoon, I discovered the elixir which seemed to wash away the awful metal taste. We'd gone to our local Safeway store where they were launching a new Cragmont grapefruit pop. Samples were being offered in the store. Because it was tart and acidic with a strong flavor, it cut through the metal shield like a knife. I was soon drinking two or three cans a day. Although it hurt briefly going down my esophagus because of the acid content, it was a wonderful, refreshing drink. We should have bought shares in Cragmont.

The distasteful metallic sensation usually lasted a week or so after each treatment, then tapered off. I was then able to enjoy all drinks for at least two weeks a month.

Journal entry: Sunday May 1. it's been tough
getting over the second chemo session. My
stomach has been so upset. The mornings
are usually pretty good, but the evenings are
troublesome. The numbness is especially acute
in my fingers and toes this time around. It's
very frustrating, but I must learn to ignore it.
I ate quite a bit and am using the juicer that
Caroline bought a few days ago. Carrot juice is
absolutely ugly to drink, I don't know if I'll ever
get to like that stuff. Maybe I should try mixing
it with other vegetables.

(Sunday night; 11 p.m.) I'm still going in too
many directions at the same time. I want to
start finishing the garage and bring home our
62 Chevy from Lloyd's farm later this year.

*There are so many things I want to get done
right away but I have to restrain myself. I have
to look after me first.*

I'd been so busy over the past couple of decades with so many different projects outside of radio and TV. I'd worked at two jobs, twelve hours a day for five years in Lethbridge, teaching broadcasting at the Lethbridge Community College and hosting the morning show on CJOC radio. I knew it would take time to formulate a new way of thinking and begin to slow down. But for me, it was easier said than done.

Then a profound, significant and pivotal event occurred in my cancer journey as I entered my third month of treatments. One of Caroline's friends at the Bank of Montreal, Joan Heila gave us a copy of Dr. Bernie Siegel's book, "Love, Medicine and Miracles". He's a renowned American oncologist who believes a combination of medicine, faith and a positive attitude were crucial in helping to overcome serious illnesses. Dr. Siegel wrote:

> "Many people fear that encouraging patients to take responsibility for their own health and emotions will make them feel like failures if they can't cure themselves. That is missing the point. We are asking people to play an active part in their health care. NOT DEMANDING of them that they get well. Exceptional patients don't try not to die. They try to live until they die. Then they are successes no matter what the outcome of the diseases".

Dr. Siegel spoke of "exceptional cancer patients", or ECP's, who live by the above example which was a source of tremendous strength for me. He preached the importance of visualization, and at the end of his book, diagrammed in detail how to center myself and allow my mind to become a positive force in dealing with my cancer.

Whenever I could, during my lunch breaks and on weekends, I lay on my bed and closed my eyes. With deep breathing and some practice, I was able to slow down my heart rate and relax. I centered myself right in the middle of my chest and imagined a ray of light to be the source of life and power within me.

Dr. Siegel had recommend I visualize images of strength to help me deal with my cancer journey. I concentrated on awakening the sleeping force within me from which I could draw the power to help me in my fight for life. I conjured up a vision of myself dressed in a glistening suit of impenetrable armor, on a brilliant white horse. In my hand was a giant, gleaming amber-colored sword that flashed with streaks of lightening when I swung it over my head. I commanded my steed to gallop at full speed through my arteries and veins. Together we thundered through my bloodstream, slicing in half, each ugly, twisted cancer cell we encountered. I speared the remnants with the tip of the sword and flung them into a deep, dark, hole; into hell itself where I witnessed them being instantly vaporized.

Slowly, day after day, I lay on my bed and imagined myself eradicating the insidious, creeping, life-sucking parasites from within my body in a blinding firestorm of rage.

It was a rage I counted on as part of the equation in helping save my life.

Chapter 11

I NEVER CONSCIOUSLY ASKED *why me* but still wondered sometimes why I had cancer.

The answer came through graphically in Dr. Siegel's book. He talked about the disease as a gift. *A gift?* I wondered incredulously. *Cancer?*

One of his female patients had written in the midst of chemotherapy and radiation treatments:

> "I consider my cancer to be such a blessing because through it we have learned so much about how to handle our lives, how to speak to each other, how we acknowledge our feelings about each other; how we throw away the junk forever and have more contentment in our lives.

One particular phrase stuck with me. *How we throw away the junk forever.* I used to be bothered by petty, insignificant things or events out of my control. I would tune in to the news each day and listen to 'junk' and let it fester. *No more.* As my buddy Paul Willis once told me 25 years earlier, "don't sweat the small stuff" It took my cancer journey to understand what he meant.

Dr. Siegel described another cancer patient, a 22 year old man who wrote:

"I've learned to live. I love living. I love my family, my friends, my job. Every day I wake up, I feel alive …at peace. Please excuse this outburst. I get carried away sometimes. I've been dealing with cancer for more than a year now. I'm almost glad I got it. It's changed my whole outlook on living. I LIVE from day to day. I make the most out of each day!

My eyes widened as I read and was breathless when I finished his story. The blinders seemed to fall from my eyes as I read that last sentence in the paragraph over and over again and I knew I would never again feel sorry for myself.

…I make the most out of every day.

That account of the young man's thoughts stayed with me for the rest of my cancer journey. To this day, I don't know if he survived or not but I wished I could've met him. I received an enormous amount of courage and inspiration from what he said.

In another story, Dr. Siegel recounted how a colleague of his who was chairing a workshop told him about a 50 year old woman who had a double mastectomy. She spoke to the gathering at her doctor's request.

"Three years ago I was graced with cancer. I searched my whole life for a teacher, and it wasn't until I was diagnosed that I really started to pay attention to the preciousness of each breath, to the momentum of each thought, until I saw that this very moment in time is all that I have. All my other teachers gave me ideas. My cancer caused me to directly experience my life. When I was diagnosed, it was up to me to be reborn before I died.

IT WAS UP TO ME TO BE RE-BORN BEFORE I DIED!

The spirituality of it all sunk in. It was like starting a new life! A second chance.

It was up to me to throw away all my judgments and petty dislikes and to live life to it's fullest. Again my eyes fell on the prophetic words of the anonymous writer, "...it wasn't until I was diagnosed that I really started to pay attention to the preciousness of each breath, the momentum of each thought".

I knew it would be my response to the cancer and the treatments that was the most important tool in my arsenal to eradicate the cancer in my body.

Mac Davis wrote in the early 70's, "you gotta stop and smell the roses".

I promised myself I would lose the 'junk'.

> *Journal entry: May 5. In spite of the spiritual awakenings in Dr. Siegel's book, today was the harshest day so far because of the numbness in my fingers and toes. Today was also a write-off in terms of work. I didn't do much. I'm even having trouble holding my pen as I write this. I'm hoping the next couple of weeks will be better because I'm done with the steroids for now.*

The Prednizone caused my sleep patterns to be altered. I was told at the clinic many people suffered from insomnia and mood swings from the effects of the drug. I didn't seem to suffer from any mood alterations but found I did not sleep well. They caused me to enter a vicious cycle of 'uppers and downers'.

For fourteen days each cycle, I took the steroids twice a day and two Ativan tablets at bedtime to relax. Often though, when I closed my eyes to try to sleep, a laser light show erupted in my head. Like a scene from a video game, lightening bolts streaked and flashed wildly inside my skull. Bursts of colors and fireworks exploded behind my eyes. It was a visual spectacle any world class rock band would've been proud of. Coupled with the pyrotechnical display was the dull roar of unidentifiable sounds that pounded in my ears. I felt a rush of blood in my temples with each corresponding heartbeat and at times, my heart seemed to race. I tried to visualize slowing down the thumping in my chest, but to no avail. To bring on sleep, I often got up in the middle of the night and stumbled into the bathroom, opened the prescription bottle containing the sleeping pills and swallowed two.

Back in bed, watching the soft yellow numbers on our digital alarm clock beside me tick the minutes away, I waited for the darkness to smother the spectacular light show and mute the cacophony of sound. Eventually I sank into an unnatural, drug induced oblivion.

In the mornings, I often woke up with a hangover. The light and noise was gone and the black coffee helped clear some of the cobwebs. I was buffeted from feeling exhausted; to being calm, then wired; to being in and out of control - sometimes all at the same time.

> *Journal entry: May 6. Well, the decision was made to go on long term disability after meeting with Ralph Robinson today. I told him I could no longer give 100 percent in my job. I was not benefiting myself or the radio station anymore. It's going to be interesting to see how I'm able to spend my time now that I'm going to have a lot more of it. I do not feel any different in terms of no longer being the bread winner in the family. I have to be selfish; to look after myself first now. I have to do it for my family.*

For the first time in 24 years of uninterrupted work, I was on the shelf as I walked out of the front door that afternoon. I had said my good-byes to my friends at the station and they wished me well. Just before I left my office, I scanned the room.

There were sales graphs and charts pinned to the wall above my desk. They indicated my selling records from month-to-month. I slowly placed my personal items into my briefcase as well as the pictures of the kids and Caroline and me. We'd had it taken by a friend in Lethbridge a year earlier. The four of us were dressed casually, smiling and seemingly with not a care in the world. I put the picture carefully into my briefcase to make sure the glass didn't break and closed it up.

As I shut the front door behind me and took a few steps, I stopped on the sidewalk in front of the station. I took a long, last look and got choked up. I moved quickly to our car parked at the curb and walked past the parking meter with the 'expired' flag up, unlocked the door and placed my brief-case in the back seat. Opening the driver's door, I slumped down like a sack of rocks in a heap behind the steering wheel. Time stood still. I let my fingers rest on the wheel. My mind tried to grasp the enormity of what had just happened.

I don't have a job anymore and I sure hope I qualify for long term disability.

I was completely oblivious to the traffic passing by me on the left, I didn't notice the pedestrians on the right. People entered and exited the CIGV front door. I didn't see or hear anything. Again and again, like an audio tape on a continu-ous loop without an end, my mind was riveted on only one thought.

I...DON'T...HAVE...A...JOB...ANYMORE!

I sat as still as a stone until I was jolted back to reality when someone in a car driving by me suddenly accelerated which startled me. I started the car and put it in gear and moved into the driving lane from the curb. I slowed down before the stop sign at the end of the street. I couldn't shake the deflation, the terror of being unemployed. I stared at myself in the rear view mirror. No smile. No hair. The driver behind me hit his horn. I looked quickly both ways and turned left.

Idiot. I muttered to myself and sped up the avenue.

I got home and walked up the slight incline to the front door. Someone had given Caroline a ride home and she greeted me. We exchanged kisses. "How do you feel?" she asked sympathetically. I paused for a moment.

"I really don't know".

"Are you going to be okay?"

"I think so".

That night as I tried to sleep again, the blizzard of questions intensified. We had just bought our home.

Should we have?

How in heaven's sake can we afford the payments?

Can we cancel the deal?

I don't have a job.

Caroline is only working part time.

There are four of us to feed.

Insurance in this province is so bloody expensive.

Our house was almost paid for in Lethbridge.

Now we have a big mortgage again.

We had a ton of friends back home.

Here we don't know many people.

I have cancer.

Was the move a mistake?

For the first time since we left southern Alberta, doubts pounded into my mind about the wisdom of the relocation especially since I was the one who had driven the decision to move. My heart sank as I reached over and touched Caroline's hip. She was asleep.

"Please forgive me for taking you away from your family and friends", I pleaded softly, not wanting to wake her. "I'm so sorry honey. You're going to have to continue to be strong for all of us now."

I snuggled as close as I could without waking her. Again, as it would for the duration of my chemotherapy protocol, sleep did not come for a long time that night.

Chapter 12

*Journal entry: May 8. Mother's Day. Didn't
do much. I'm really bothered by the numbness
now. The drugs are still irritating my stomach
lining as well. I'm dealing with a constant
upset stomach. I really wish I could enjoy this
beautiful weather to the fullest. However, the
more I read Dr. Siegel's book, the more I am
determined to fight back – hard. I will not give
in to this. <u>There will be better days and times
ahead</u>.*

I HAD JUST FINISHED two complete cycles. Four pokes. Four
times the chemicals had coursed through my bloodstream.
The baldness, upset stomach and numbing of the fingertips
and toes had taken firm hold. I'd come to know what to expect from each treatment and what was to come after.

Ralph called me on Sunday evening and asked me to say
good-bye to my clients in Oliver and Osoyoos and to tidy up
any loose business ends

I got into our car at 8 a.m. Monday May 9th and headed
down highway 97 toward Osoyoos, 45 miles away, a community of five thousand people right on the U.S. border.
I intentionally left the air conditioning off and opened all
the windows in the car. I wanted to absorb the magnificent
beauty and smells of the orchards in spring bloom in the

Okanagan, one of the most beautiful places in the country.

I drove along east side road beside Skaha Lake toward Okanagan Falls on my way to the town of Oliver, about halfway to Osoyoos. The ribbon of asphalt snaked by the water, then cut through the miles of orchards on both sides of the road.

I witnessed the explosion of pink and white blossoms mixed with the green leaves. The delicious fragrance of the petals wafted throughout the car. I breathed in deeply, to fill every air sac with the overpowering, sweet smell.

I did however, miss the rush of wind through my hair. I rubbed the stubble on my scalp in a vain attempt to remember what it felt like.

I dropped into each of my client's business and told them why I was on sick leave. They were surprised, some were shocked when I told them of the Hodgkin's. Each one wished me good luck. I ate a late lunch on the patio of an outdoor café in Osoyoos, then hit the road for the return trip home, experiencing again the same euphoric rush as I did in the morning.

I played a couple of my cassettes. Each song took me back to where I was thirty years earlier. I tried to remember what I was doing and where I was when each song was a hit.

Over supper, I talked about my last day of work at Great Valleys Radio with Caroline, Jodi and Chris. I didn't know how to express my feelings of not working, because I had never been unemployed since starting work at my dad's bakery in Calgary when I was in my early teens.

That night, as I tried to fall asleep, I was deeply disturbed by what had transpired.

A nagging thought kept tugging at my mind. *You haven't been working for a full six months.* I remembered from my initial discussion at the time I was hired that long-term disability was only available if I passed my probation and was employed for at least a half-year. At the time, I never thought it might be an issue because I didn't know that cancer had already invaded my body. The thought that I might not be eligible for assistance was deeply troubling.

> *Journal entry: May 10. I went back to the*
> *station and applied for long-term medical*
> *disability. I was nervous about it because of*
> *the mandatory six month term of employment*
> *clause. Mary told me she would do her best*
> *to forward my claim but couldn't promise*
> *anything.*

I continued to be bothered by the time frame and kept thinking I should have tried to stay on for another month, but considering my condition, I didn't see how that was possible.

As I drove back home, I thought about the budget discussions Caroline and I had a few days earlier. We knew we had to re-arrange our entire financial situation to compensate for me not working. Money would be very tight. We even talked about the possibility of having to dip into our RRSP's. By the time the bi-weekly mortgage was paid and groceries bought, there wasn't much left. Gasoline was a precious commodity.

Caroline had applied for a permanent full-time position at the bank and we were told it was only a matter of time before something came up. Chris could only work part time at Safeway because he was finishing grade twelve, and Jodi had a couple of shifts at Burger King on the weekends.

We had a family discussion on our predicament. The kids said they would chip in whatever they could. Caroline reassured us that everything would be alright. But I could see behind her façade. She was worried.

As I lay in bed that night, my body both tingling and numb, I tried to be and think positively. I couldn't escape from one thought however, that tightened the knot in my stomach.

What if we lose our home?

> *Journal entry: May 11. I have always been*

proud of my physical shape. For the past 15
years I've kept myself in excellent condition. I
even found out I was in better shape than 95
percent of men my age in a fitness test in 1992
when I was teaching in Lethbridge. Will this
factor into my fighting this monstrosity? Time
will tell, I guess.

What I saw in the mirror was almost comical. My stubby head, thinning mustache, shrinking upper body and expanding middle made me look like a reject from a nerd film.

My chest muscles had disappeared as they atrophied. My biceps were smaller and my collarbones were starkly visible. My ribs were painfully exposed, putting an xylophone to shame. My stomach was enlarged. I stared at the grotesque shape.

This isn't the <u>real</u> me.

I tried not to stare, but found myself transfixed at the bloated image. I was shocked by the physiological changes. I so wished I could hop on my bike and ride to the gym to attack the weights. But I knew I could not begin on the restoration of my beleaguered body for at least six long months.

Journal entry: Saturday May 14. I see more and
more antique and classic cars and trucks on the
streets, especially on the weekends. Gee, I wish I
had my old car here. It would look so good with
the others here in the south Okanagan.

I was convinced somewhere deep in the bowels of the valley, someone was building old 1960's Mustangs. I'd never seen so many and all beautifully restored. I had a strong urge to bring back my old classic. I put that on my mental "to-do" list, once I got better and began earning money again.

Journal entry: May 17. Well, here we go again.

*Tomorrow I begin the first session of the third
cycle. Although I've only completed two, it
feels longer than that. Time seems to drag so
slowly…yet, I'm about to start the third set of
pokes. I travelled to Kelowna today after being
granted an interview with the program manager
at the TV station to check out the possibility
of voicing some commercials. It might lead to
something and would certainly help financially.*

I drove to Kelowna to meet with the manager. I had over
twenty years experience in voicing radio and TV spots and I
had hoped I could get some free lance work. He was cordial
and sympathetic, but had nothing available at that moment.
I left copies of audio and video tapes of some of my previous
work and thanked him for his time.

*Journal entry: May 19. (10 a.m.) Second day
after the first session of cycle three. Didn't feel
too badly. Mornings are always better than the
evenings. It's probably from force-feeding myself
all day long. I feel like exploding at times from
all the food I'm trying to cram into my stomach.
I'm surprised, however, that my weight has
remained steady around 150 pounds. (8 p.m.)
I'm back at the books studying for my C.R.A.
final. Tough to concentrate at times. I'm hoping
I feel as well next Thursday as I do today. If
so, the trip back to Lethbridge should go quite
smoothly. But first, it's time to get prepared for
our company who will arrive this weekend.*

We were expecting a number of relatives for the Victoria Day
weekend. My sister Ann Palmer and her husband Percy were flying from Edmonton. Caroline's sister Rose Neufeld and husband
Dave were driving from Coaldale, a few miles east of Lethbridge.
We were excited at the thought of being together again.

The last time we'd seen them was during our move from southern Alberta.

Two months earlier, I'd registered for the Certified Radio Advisor diploma course as part of the requirements of my job description. It was a correspondence course sponsored by the Radio Marketing Bureau in Toronto which would benefit me once I was back in sales. I had done the assignments on the days I felt well. The final exam was scheduled in the middle of June.

I checked the calendar. It was to take place a day after a poke.

While all that was going on, we were also in the process of preparing for our first visit back to Lethbridge since our move. The excitement grew as the days got closer to our journey back to Alberta. Chris had planned for several months to attend the graduation of his grade 12 class at the Lethbridge Collegiate Institute. He'd known most of his friends as far back as kindergarten.

He was quite upset when we informed him of our move to B.C. just as he started his final high school year and Jodi was equally appalled at leaving her friends. Caroline and I had given Chris the option of staying in Lethbridge with our friends or relatives to graduate with his friends. However, after much discussion with us and soul searching on his part, he reluctantly chose to move with us and transferred with his sister to Penticton Secondary School.

Caroline and I were immensely relieved when he made the decision. I couldn't imagine what it would have been like to have him living more than 500 miles away from us. We were always a close family and to have him that far away when dealing with cancer would have made the situation unbearable.

On May 20th, Caroline and I drove to the airport to pick up my sister and her husband. We watched in eager anticipation as their plane landed. Ann and I ran to each other after she'd cleared security and embraced in the middle of the waiting area. We held each other tightly. I thanked her for coming to see me as I wiped the tears from her face. We gathered up her luggage and headed home.

Dave and Rose arrived a couple of hours later by car and a similar tearful outburst occurred at that time between Caroline and her sister. The six of us spent the rest of the day reminiscing and swapping stories. We called my brother Conrad in Calgary who had also hoped to see us for the weekend. But because he and his wife Barb had several small children, they were not able to travel as freely as the others.

It was wonderful to re-establish family ties over supper. It was the kind of emotional uplifting we so desperately needed. After dinner, we drove to the Burger King to visit Jodi and had ice creams together. We then headed to Skaha Lake and walked in the shallow water at the beach, chatting endlessly.

With everyone sleeping that night, I got up at 1 a.m. and picked up Jodi at the restaurant after her shift. She was only 15 and didn't have her driver's license.

"You smell like a hamburger", I teased as she got into the car. She told me that joke got to be stale after a while. We listened to the radio and talked a bit on the five minute drive back to our house.

Before we knew it, the weekend had zipped by and two days later we were back at the airport saying goodbye to Ann and Percy.

> Journal entry: May 23. Percy and Ann flew
> back to Edmonton yesterday and Dave and Rose
> later left for Victoria. Before they drove away,
> the four of us stood in a circle and held hands.
> Dave offered a prayer for my recovery and for
> strength. I felt God's presence.

On Thursday the 24th, I had my second poke in cycle three.

The following day we left for Lethbridge, traveling east on Highway 3 toward Alberta in two vehicles for a visit to our old home town. Jodi and Chris were in his newly-purchased 1983 Z-28 Camaro and Caroline and me in our well-worn 1972 Chev pickup.

We stopped only for gasoline, bathroom breaks and a quick lunch in Creston.

Even in my altered state, I still loved to drive, especially in the mountains. When we lived on the prairies, we'd often visited the Okanagan for vacations, usually once every two years.

The sun was settling on the western horizon when our mini-convoy wheeled up in front of Caroline sister's house in north Lethbridge. Garry and Deanna Peacock had lived there for fifteen years. Chris drove away to show his new wheels to his old school mates.

Over wine and snacks, the rest of us talked until midnight, catching up on the latest news from the city in which we'd lived for seventeen years.

My baldness was also a topic of discussion.

> *Journal entry: May 27. Caroline and I spent Saturday and Sunday visiting friends. She met with former colleagues at the Bank of Montreal where she'd spent all her working time in the city. I knew her mascara would take a real beating. I visited Barry at his store and we swapped stories about our old Chevys. Time passed quickly and it was suppertime before we knew it. That night we went out for more visitations. I don't think I'll get much sleep over the next few days.*

We'd been long-time friends with Barry and Karen Fritz who owned a paint store in the downtown area. Barry and I had founded Chinook Chevys in the mid 80's. Our families and the dozen other members had traveled to many classic car conventions in western Canada and the United States.

So many friends to see in such little time. Exhausted, we went to bed about 1 a.m.

We were awakened two hours later. Chris was at the foot of our bed. In the swirling fog in my head, I heard him softly say, "Mom, I just wrecked my car."

We bolted upright in bed.

Chapter 13

MY HEART LEAPT INTO my throat. "Are you okay?" we both asked simultaneously. I tried to shake the cobwebs from my head, trying to grasp the reality of what we'd just heard. I wasn't sure if I'd imagined it or not.

He and his friend were all right. They'd been visiting with others from his former grade twelve graduating class. His sports car was in a collision downtown with a 4X4 pickup truck with oversized tires. The truck won.

Caroline and I both embraced our son, trying to comfort him. I felt absolutely sick for Chris. I told him I once smashed a 1962 convertible when I was 18, trying to relate my experience with what had just happened. I was hoping he would talk and let the emotions come to the surface.

But he remained quiet, his 6'1" frame hunched over, not responding. I could tell he was crushed. He'd worked so hard over the previous three years to save money for the Z-28. We continued to hold him tightly, rocking slowly back and forth. In the still darkness of that small bedroom I totally forgot about my own struggle.

We broke our embrace and I suggested he go to bed and try to get some sleep. He got up and slowly walked to the bedroom door, his stooped shoulders speaking volumes about his loss. We felt so sorry for him.

Journal entry: May 28. We went to a barbeque

at the home of Carol and Rome Thibert, whom
we'd known for over 25 years. Many of our
closest friends were there too. I don't know if
I can put it into words what it was like going
back to visit them. How is it possible in six
months to leave behind the memory of a city
full of friends and family after 17 years? It feels
like we'd been gone much longer. I'm hoping
I haven't deceived myself into believing that
all those years, despite what has happened in
the last half-year, doesn't mean anything. The
roots are simply too deep, right to our very
core. At three in the morning, they gave us an
unexpected gift. An envelope filled with cash.
This is what real, caring friendship is all about;
real caring, real love.

When we opened that envelope, I could have felt like a welfare recipient. The opposite, however was true. Because it came from our best friends, it was the ultimate and generous act; unconditional love and caring. The kind of love that spells it out without uttering a word. In the past, I'd often kept my feelings and emotions to myself, under control, not letting them come to the surface.

But after three months of chemotherapy, I had become pretty good at crying. The pent-up emotions, restrained over so many years, had been blown away to set the torrent of tears free. In that tight circle of love and emotion, our foreheads touching and tears mingling, I cried with Caroline as we were embraced by our friends. Later that morning, about four o'clock as we were getting ready for bed I wrote in my journal:

My mask is now removed. I am not afraid to
show my vulnerability. It is not important to
be the bread-winner in my family anymore – to

*put up a façade, to be something I'm not. We
can and must rely on our friends for their love
and support for everything, especially their
friendship. Friendship – this has to be one of the
most beautiful words in the world. Especially
deep-rooted, everlasting love where distances
shrink in time of trouble. I thank God for our
friends.*

I awoke when Chris came in two hours later. He'd been at an all-night safe grad party with his high school buddies on the outskirts of town. He smelled like he'd been roasted over an open fire. Dead-tired, he climbed into his sleeping bag on the basement carpet. It wasn't long before he was snoring.

Garry had breakfast ready about 9 a.m. For the third consecutive night, we'd only slept a few hours which concerned me. I'd been warned by the oncology nurses to get plenty of rest. *Tomorrow. I'll rest tomorrow.*

We had a whole city full of friends to see in only two days. I swore to myself I'd catch up on my sleep back home.

We arrived at McKillop United Church on Sunday morning just before the 10:30 service and became re-acquainted with more old friends. It felt good again to be sitting on the left side of the sanctuary, in the same pew a dozen rows from the front. For thirteen years, we'd occupied those seats while listening to Reverends Alex Lawson and Ross White.

Just before we left Lethbridge that afternoon for our trip northward to Calgary and home on the Trans Canada Highway, Chris and I climbed into Garry's pickup and took a drive to see the Camaro at his friend's body shop lot. My son stood silently by his car.

The front end had been pushed twelve inches to the passenger side from the impact of the collision when the truck had hit the side at 90 degrees. Both fenders were crumpled, the hood twisted like the lid of a newly opened can of sardines and the left front wheel was bent over.

We slowly walked around it, Chris behind us dragging his feet in the gravel.

He was hunched over again, his hands deep in the pockets of his jeans and his ball cap low on his forehead. Garry and I tried to make light of the accident but he was not in a smiley mood. We took a couple of photographs before we left. He looked over his shoulder wistfully through the back window of the truck at his wounded baby. Garry offered to get the sports car repaired. We thanked him and agreed one of us would return to Lethbridge to drive it back to Penticton when the repairs were done.

A half-hour later, the four of us crammed into our truck. The back was packed full with the remainder of our belongings that we'd left behind at the time of our original move. Chris was quiet much of the trip, as we headed north toward Carmangay, a farming town of several hundred people in the middle of the vast southern Alberta prairie. We arrived at Lloyd and Colleen Annabel's farm, 35 miles north of Lethbridge where my antique car was stored. Lloyd and I share a fondness for old Chevs, especially those with the fabled 409. He'd been a drag racer in the 60's and 70's and was an expert in assembling the engines. Mine needed some work and he had rebuilt it over the previous winter.

We visited for a couple of hours and I drove my old muscle car back and forth on his driveway a few times. It felt so good to hear the rumble of the dual exhausts when I fired it up. I told him I would return with a trailer later in the summer to take the car back with me.

We drove to Calgary as evening fell and stayed at the home of Caroline's sister and husband, Donna and Ross Brown. The following morning at seven, we were on the road again for home. The old truck groaned and creaked under it's load all the way back to the Okanagan Valley. The trip gave us plenty of time to sift through our thoughts. We chatted about memories of our time with family and friends in Lethbridge and talked candidly about spiritual matters and how important our faith was at that time in our lives.

We were serious, thoughtful, reflective and funny, all at the same time.

As well, with the four of us squished on the seat, it was the ultimate test of underarm deodorant endurance. We'd also made a pact the previous day, not to eat beans or vegetables prone to cause gas for at least 24 hours.

Weary and bleary-eyed, we pulled up in front of our house eleven hours later. We decided to unpack the truck the following morning so we parked it directly under the streetlight in front of our house, locked the doors and stumbled in the front entrance of our home. It didn't take long for Caroline and the kids to nod off.

As exhausted as I was, I couldn't get to sleep, the adrenaline kept me from slumber and my stomach had started to churn again. A few hours later, in the middle of the night, I got out of bed, found my journal, and in the soft glow of the lamp by the sofa, I again put more thoughts on paper.

> *Journal entry: May 30. Pretty bleak night.*
> *This is the roughest I've felt for quite a while.*
> *Probably the coming down from the Prednizone,*
> *the exhaustion of the trip, the sore stomach, the*
> *numbness: all of the above. It doesn't help either*
> *that I'm taking all of these bloody pills – the*
> *'uppers' and 'downers' don't make me feel well*
> *at all. I seem void of any energy. My stomach*
> *has started to really kick up again, much like the*
> *time I had to go on the Zytotech. My throat is*
> *also sore but I don't think I have an infection.*
> *Last month my pulse was higher when my chest*
> *was sore.*

My fingers and toes were almost completely numb. At times, they were absolutely useless. I couldn't pick up small objects and if I needed to write something, I'd have to slide a pen or pencil across the table with one hand and drop it into the other.

Coins were impossible to pick up from a flat surface and I couldn't button up my shirts. If we went out somewhere, Caroline would have to tie my shoes, put the belt through the loops in the pants, then buckle it up. She even had to zip up the fly. Knives and forks were also a real challenge. I had to pick them up, using all fingers and thumbs. Tasks which I took for granted in the past, had become laborious. My fingers felt as if tight, tiny rubber bands had been placed around the first joint of each digit, cutting off the circulation.

I experienced another phenomenon with my chemically altered fingers. Like the sound in stereo headphones, reverberating from side-to-side, the feeling of numbness intensified in one or two fingertips, then subsided. The odd sensation was often repeated in the other hand.

Left to right, then back again. From tingling to total numbness. The unexplained medical oddity caused my fingers to twitch and hurt. Intense, quick stabs of pain flashed intermittently into the tips – then just as quickly, they'd be devoid of any feeling. At other times, like a balloon being squeezed, my fingertips felt like they were about to explode, the blood pounding against the inside of them.

I referred continually to Dr. Siegel's book which helped me through the rough times.

He challenged cancer patients to look at chemotherapy as something beneficial, something life-giving. I re-read about visualization; to 'see' the cancer cells and watch them being choked off or cut in half. I tried to think of the side-effects as a result of positive changes happening within me. As in physics, for every action there is a reaction.

With chemotherapy, it had to be the same for me. There was a reaction and certainly there was cell damage. The first damage from the cancer and the second from the chemicals.

The side effects were stark reminders of the changes occurring within me.

In a strange and convoluted way, the second damage was making me better, only it would still take several months to see if there would be the outcome we hoped for.

Two days of late spring rains made it hard not to let my attitude be compromised by the gray, overcast skies. I opened my textbooks to take my mind off things. I'd been studying in spite of my discomfort to be ready for my final exam. The toughest times to concentrate were the days immediately following a poke. In college, I'd written tests while hung-over or fighting a cold or the flu. The C.R.A. final would prove not to be the same.

> *Journal entry: June 7. Felt good today – as close to normal as I've felt for a long time, but this has happened before. In a week I go for my fourth cycle and then I'm halfway done. Hard to believe, isn't it? Something else has happened which I don't like. I'm having trouble focusing my eyes at times. Much of what I look at has fuzzy edges. Dr. Chritchley told me it was probably another chemo side-effect.*

> *Journal entry: June 8. As I read more of Dr. Siegel, I realize I'm treading too softly. I must be more aggressive. If I get angry, that's okay. It certainly won't make me any sicker than I am. The dark thoughts that creep into my consciousness are natural, but I will fight hard to replace them with positive thoughts of what the future holds for me.*

Over the previous few weeks I had started to withdraw, taking it easy and not pushing myself at all. I felt I had to rest and not do anything that could cause stress and injury.

It seemed I was constantly tugged between following the advice of the oncology nursing staff and my desire to throw it all out the window and get active again. I'd quit doing anything strenuous. The carport sat idle, waiting to be enclosed with walls and a roof. The old pickup was quietly rusting away. I felt like an imprisoned couch potato.

I gave myself a mental spanking and promised to get active again. I was determined to fight through the nausea, upset stomach, weakness and malaise I experienced. I vowed to not walk on eggshells any longer.

Caroline and I got back on our mountain bikes and tried to ride at least a half-hour each day. I continued to educate myself and read more books and articles about fighting cancer and the importance of a positive attitude.

I had to be careful not to think too much. I was philosophizing and arguing with myself. At the same time, I knew it was crucial to continue to explore my thoughts and feelings so I could understand how I felt as I did and to fight hard not to allow the sinister thoughts to creep in.

I also worked at being at peace with myself, to further explore my spirituality and to take it to a new plateau of comfort and strength. I decided it was okay to have a 'down day' and to take advantage of the good days, to take them to new highs and heights.

> *Journal entry: June 14. The New York Rangers won the Stanley Cup tonight. I must be one of the few people in BC who are pleased about it. I have to be careful not to rub it in to anyone who is a Canuck fan. They reminded me at the clinic about that fact. I don't heal as quickly as I used to.*

Chapter 14

Journal entry: June 15. I found out today I was not eligible for long term disability. I'm stunned. Three weeks short of qualifying. And even if I was, there was no guarantee I would have been able to collect benefits because Dr. Chritchley had determined I had cancer long before I was diagnosed. The helplessness is overwhelming. I have no idea how we are going to make it without a job or disability income. What now? I lie on top of our bed after a forced mid-day nap and look around the bedroom; at the drapes that I looked at yesterday and the day before that, and the day before that. The clothes closet, the ceiling fan, mirror on Caroline's dresser. My pile of car magazines on the floor by my night table. The sun peeking through the crack at the bottom of the drawn blind. Nothing changes. Time is standing still. My life, like a video tape horror movie in a VCR has been put on 'pause'.

WHEN MARY FERRIER, THE accountant at the station, sympathetically told me the insurance company rejected my claim, I was crushed. Fear and panic welled up inside me. Thoughts of losing our home scared me to death. *What about food; and gasoline; and insurance.* I'd taken them all for granted in the past. The necessities suddenly loomed like huge obstacles. *How are we ever going to make it?* Again, I agonized over the move to Penticton a few months earlier.

Did we do the right thing?

No. The question was, *did I do the right thing? With me being so ill, wouldn't we have been better off back in the comfortable surroundings we'd known for almost two decades?*

Our friends and relatives would have been there for support. My family had been perfectly content to live in Lethbridge. Life was good; it was grand. Then suddenly, out of the blue, I got the idea we should move. Had I thought of the consequences carefully?

Was I thinking only of myself without taking into account the feelings and wishes of my family?

My world had come to a crashing, grinding halt. The unknown of fighting cancer made it even more frightening, especially without an income. Never in 24 years of work did I ever, in my wildest dreams, think it was to come to that. The cold, hard fact smacked me squarely in the face. For the first time in my life, I would have to rely on someone or something other than myself to keep paying the bills and putting food on the table.

> *Journal entry: June 16. Woke up weak,*
> *physically, mentally and spiritually drained. I*
> *had only one choice. Unemployment Insurance.*
> *I would have to apply for U.I. Would I be*
> *eligible? "Unemployment Insurance", the*
> *words recoil through my brain. I hate those two*
> *words.*

> *Journal entry: June 16.(9 pm) Felt rotten today.*
> *More from my pride taking a battering than*
> *anything else. I feel useless, dirty, unclean.*
> *There's an old country song that I can't shake*

*from my mind. It's called "Waiting in the
Welfare Line". I keep telling myself 'somehow,
someway we have to do whatever we can as a
family to pay the mortgage and buy groceries.
We don't have a choice. We're also going to have
to cash in some RRSP's to make it through until
I can get back to work.*

I drove downtown that morning and found a parking
space near the Unemployment Insurance office on Ellis Street.
As long as I live, I will never forget what it felt like standing
in line, waiting for my turn to speak with an agent. In the
midst of those dozen people being processed, I felt isolated,
ashamed and so very alone.

As I looked about nervously, hoping I didn't see anyone
I knew, I thought of the many people who knew me from
my work in radio and television in Lethbridge over 17 years.
I was often stopped on the street or in stores by those who
saw my television weathercasts or listened to my morning radio show. They told me their stories which I often related on
the air. I'd met most big country recording stars like Kenny
Rogers, Alabama, Sawyer Brown and Dwight Yoakum and
MC'd their concerts. They came back annually and I got to
know them and their band members on a first-name basis. I
often hung out with them after the shows.

I have a picture of Wayne Gretzky and me when he was
in Lethbridge at the unveiling of new shopping center which
he bought in 1982. I spent the afternoon interviewing him
for my radio station. I was on top of the world and life was
wonderful.

I was a local celebrity.

Less than a year later, it was over. Like a wonderful, fan-
tasy filled movie, the credits were rolling as the lights went
down. I was skirting to stay out of the grave, drawn and haggard, unemployed, unknown and at the mercy of the system.

I looked around the room. Nobody was smiling. Some

were bored, others edgy, but most seemed resigned to their fate of looking for work. There was a time I'd looked down in disdain at those on welfare or U.I. *Have they no pride,* I used to think.

What a bunch of bums, milking the system. Now I was one of those 'bums' and the milk was sour. I hated being in that government office.

Following a lengthy wait, I finally met with a U.I officer. After taking some information, and looking at several options, she told me I was eligible for 15 weeks of U.I. medical assistance. I signed the necessary documents and was told I'd get my first cheque in a couple of weeks. Twice a month I would receive $374, a pittance of what I had earned in the past.

My confidence took a massive hit. There didn't seem to be a way out of the physical and mental prison walls that grew a little higher each day. What frightened me most of all, was waking up each morning knowing exactly what would happen that day. Like a one-act play encompassing 24-hours, I was condemned to repeat the frightening scene over and over.

It gave eternity a much more clear and distinct meaning.

Then came a phone call that seemed to make that eternity creep horribly closer.

It was 11:30 a.m., June 17th. I was watching TV at home. A couple of hours earlier, I'd gone in for my pre-chemo bloodwork. I got up from my chair in the living room to answer the phone. It was Pat, the receptionist at oncology.

"Hello Wally"

"Yes"

She paused for a moment.

"I have some bad news for you", she said in a sympathetic tone.

My heart plummeted. The blood drained from my face. Feeling faint, I grabbed the nearest chair, the rocker, and slumped down. My hand had a death-grip on the phone.

Beads of sweat formed on my forehead and I felt cold and

clammy. My mind raced.

What the hell is happening? What can possibly…?

Then it dawned on me and I sat up straight. I knew what I was about to hear.

Claire had told me months ago it might happen.

"Your white counts are too low. We can't do the treatment today. I'm sorry."

"What happens next?" I asked in a resigned tone.

"We'll take a blood sample again in five days. If the counts are up, you'll get your treatment."

"Thanks Pat. I'll see you then".

I hung up the phone, closed my eyes, slumped back again into the rocking chair and let it move backwards and forwards for a few minutes. I fought waves of panic.

Later that night, after supper, we decided we had no choice but to dip into our retirement savings. We had to turn to our RRSP's to help us make it through the difficult times until our financial situation improved dramatically.

Freedom 55 had turned into Future Uncertain.

Chapter 15

SOME HODGKIN'S PATIENTS DIE.

Not necessarily because of the cancer, but from other causes. Infection, pneumonia and a variety of complications take their toll. White counts plummet because of the devastating battering on the immune system from the chemotherapy.

The body is left defenseless against even simple illness that wouldn't affect healthy people with strong immunity.

For me, the worst that could happen, did. My white counts were only at 700 milligrams. The normal was over 4,500. My regular 28 day cycle over four months was broken. Christine had warned us before the treatments that many cancer patients were not able to complete lengthy protocols of aggressive chemotherapy. She told us some became so ill near the end of their treatments, they had to be hospitalized for the remainder.

"And some don't make it," she added in a somber tone.

I picked up the phone and called Claire. I desperately needed to talk to her. When she answered, I explained how scared and upset I was. She tried to reassure me.

"Wally, don't let this little setback affect you"

"How can I NOT let it get to me?" I asked, trying to keep my fear from growing.

"Remember, we told you earlier, that this is a very normal occurrence. It proves you are not superhuman. You should concentrate on the fact you've completed half of your treatments without incident. Not many who've endured the intensive and invasive chemotherapy you've gone through can say that. Please try not to worry,"

I heard the cheerfulness in her voice. She and the others in the clinic were so wonderful when it came to being supportive and for saying the right things at the right time.

"What happens now?" I sighed.

"What's today?" she replied. "Thursday? I'll book you in for another bloodwork on Monday – we usually wait five days for the counts to come up again and they usually do. I'm sure you'll get another poke then."

She emphasized again, "please...please try not to worry."

"Thanks Claire. I'll see you next week."

I breathed a little easier as I hung the phone in it's cradle.

Later that afternoon, I reached for my copy of "Love, Medicine and Miracles". I lay on my bed and again visualized the golden swords destroying the cancer cells. From the tiniest of veins to the largest arteries, the seek and destroy mission continued.

> *Journal entry: June 17. I got caught in a*
> *downpour while riding my bicycle this*
> *afternoon after visiting a friend on the other*
> *side of the city. I hopped into a hot bath hoping*
> *I don't catch cold. I should be okay though,*
> *because the temperature got to 28 today.*
> *Tomorrow morning at 9, I write my final exam*
> *for My CRA diploma. I hope I'm feeling okay.*

I walked into the radio station at quarter to nine the following morning and was ushered into the conference room ten minutes later where I was greeted by a woman who would administer the exam. She presented me with the papers and made sure I had a pen and pencils with me. After she finished her instructions, she wished me well, left the room and closed the door behind her.

After a three hour marathon of questions and hypothetical possibilities concerning radio sales scenarios, she returned, accepted my paper and I left for lunch. I felt confident I'd passed the examination.

When I got home, I began my usual TV channel surfing. At times I wished we had peasant television – three channels and rabbit ears. It would have made choosing the stations much easier. I usually watched CNN. I could've become a political scientist from all the hours I spent watching world events, including the OJ Simpson debacle, and couldn't believe the bizarre events as they unfolded day-to-day and week-to-week.

Father's Day arrived two days later. Armed with several empty ice cream buckets, Caroline and I drove to Vaseux Lake, a twenty minute trip south of Penticton to pick fruit. Several huge strawberry fields and cherry orchards dotted the landscape.

I was wearing a long-sleeved cotton shirt and a straw hat to keep the sun off my head. In a squat, I kept humming the old Beatles hit as we tossed the large, red, ripened berries into our containers.

It was hot, 34 degrees. I got up quickly once to pick up an empty bucket and almost keeled over. I staggered to Caroline and leaned on her shoulder. I'd suffered a major head rush and learned instantly that standing up suddenly on a scorching summer afternoon with one's blood stream full of chemicals was not a wise idea. I would have felt awfully foolish doing a face-plant into the strawberries after fainting.

I took a swig of tepid water from the plastic sports bottle I carried. After that I slowly, deliberately crouched and rose when I moved from row to row of fruit.

When we got home a couple of hours later, Jodi and Chris gave me my Father's Day gift, a pair of in-line skates. They had become a very fashionable method of transportation in the city, especially at the beaches. I put on an old hockey helmet as well as knee, elbow and wrist guards and gingerly walked across the front lawn to the pavement. Ten minutes later, I collapsed inside the front door, my face the color of the strawberries we'd picked earlier that day. I couldn't see because of the sweat and it hurt to breathe after only skating up and down the street – twice.

Plastic wheels on asphalt don't coast like blades of steel on ice. I couldn't believe how badly out of shape I was. I'm certain the road was uphill, both ways.

> *Journal entry: June 20. Day one of cycle four. My white counts were over 1500 after the morning bloodwork which meant I could have another poke. I couldn't believe how thankful I was to get another body full of chemo. I asked Dr. Chritchley how I was doing. He said he was pleased with my progress even with the five day delay. My stomach was upset all day, in anticipation of the results of the blood test. By suppertime, however, I was hungry and ate a good meal.*

> *(9:30 p.m.) I answered an ad placed in the paper today by the Penticton 1995 Summer Games Committee. They were searching for a coordinator. It paid a salary of $30,000. It seems like an enormous amount of money – especially when you're not working.*

When I met with Dr. Chritchley after the positive blood count and before the treatment, I asked him why they had dropped so dramatically after the last poke.

"It could be from a number of possibilities," he said. "Perhaps you picked up a bug of some kind that put stress on what little you have left of an immune system. Also, if you remember, I mentioned during the early part of the protocol that chemotherapy is accumulative; it doesn't dissipate like antibiotics. It might take years…and…maybe never…for your system to be free of the effects of the drugs. And remember, we're blasting you <u>really hard</u>". He emphasized the last part of his statement.

He checked his chart again and with his infectious grin, said, "whatever the problem was, is gone. Time for another poke". He gave me 'thumbs up'.

> *Journal entry: June 21. First official day of summer. The temperature hit 35 degrees. I felt fairly well, and we received some fantastic news. Caroline was offered a full time position at the bank. We celebrated by going to one of the restaurants on Okanagan Beach and bought some drinks. We walked in ankle deep water as we laughed and talked about the good news. The cool water felt so good on my hot and swollen feet.*

When Caroline called me to tell me the exciting news, I literally jumped for joy; as high as my skinny, atrophied legs could hoist me. For the first time in weeks, we didn't count our pennies. We celebrated and splurged at the cafe. She bought a colorful fruity drink and I had a banana split with extra whipping cream and hot fudge.

We talked excitedly about our good fortune and about the future, something we'd not been able to do much of in the past months. In the midst of all the hardship we'd experienced, this news came like a flashing beacon in a deep, dark eternal night. It gave us a glimmer of hope, enough to lift us up and rocket our spirits to the heavens.

There would be more joyous occasions to celebrate, at the right places and at the right times. I could sense that we were coming out of the dark valley of shadows and were at the base of the mountain, starting up the long climb to the top.

On that journey, there were still going to be times when

I'd fall backwards, but I was determined to keep the faith and only look forward.

"Here's a toast to you honey," I grinned and lifted my dish of ice cream to touch her glass which contained a small paper umbrella. I took it out and tucked it into the band on my straw hat.

"Race you to the water," I challenged her as we left the restaurant.

She beat me by a mile.

Chapter 16

As the chemotherapy became firmly entrenched, becoming part of the molecular makeup of my body, the internal functions changed. Stomach upsets were routine. Hair loss was assured. Numbness, a part of my life. Not to mention metal-mouth syndrome, muscle fatigue and atrophy.

Then came the farts. The kind that could set an elephant on it's ear or blow the neighbor's Nissan into the next block.

As I entered the fourth cycle, I noticed a definite change in the way my body was able to produce huge amounts of gas. Not the 87 octane stuff either; it was more like aviation fuel. Pizza, garlic sausage and beer used to do the trick. At that point in my treatment I got the same results from everyday ordinary foods like milk, yogurt, cheese, eggs, bread and leafy salads.

The interesting chain of events usually began with constipation shortly after each poke. Dr. Chritchley had told me before I began the treatments that the blockage was one of the side effects of the drugs. About two days after each infusion, it became difficult to have bowel movements. It was as if a stopper had been strategically placed in my backside. I tried the usual over-the-counter remedies but nothing worked immediately.

Most of the potions, pills and liquids took a few days to be effective. I got stomach cramps because of the buildup.

Once, in desperation, I tried an old remedy my mother ad-

ministered to me as a child when similar stoppages occurred
-the enema.

I was surprised at my embarrassment when I walked into
the drugstore to purchase the product. I felt as if I should be
wearing fake glasses and eyebrows with a bulbous nose. My
baldness, however, would've given away my identity – and
Caroline didn't own any wigs.

At the counter, after I'd chosen one of the enema packages,
I was relieved I didn't recognize the teenaged cashier.

*Maybe she doesn't know what this is. She only looks sixteen or
seventeen. If she asks, I'll say it's for my wife.*

This is stupid, I told myself. *It's only an enema.*

I blushed. I made sure the bag was tightly closed so no
one could see what I'd bought as I snuck out of the store like
a thief in the night. When I got home and locked myself in the
bathroom, I opened the box and studied the diagrams on the
information sheet inside the package. As a kid, I didn't have to
know about this kind of stuff because it was my mother's job
and I just had to lay face down across her lap. She had a front
row seat for the procedure and didn't need instructions.

I tried to imagine how it all would work. It seemed to me,
one had to be in good physical condition just to administer
the product to oneself. The pictures showed several positions
to be in to make insertion of the plastic tube easier. The drawings were very basic and gender-neutral. A video would have
much better to follow as a narrative described proper procedures. I tried to imagine producing the video tape instructions; or being the insertee; or the play-by-play announcer.

I started to giggle.

The plastic tube had the same ridgidness of a wet noodle
– tough to push in when a certain muscle in one's lower anatomy was tighter than a wino at midnight. Yoga would have
been far less demanding.

Nearly naked and with legs and arms splayed everywhere,
while lying between the toilet, bathtub and sink and with con-

siderable effort, I was finally able to accomplish the task.

I was exhausted. A couple of drops of sweat tumbled off my nose when I stood up on shaky legs and sat on the toilet seat.

No need to exercise. I'll just do this every night and stay in good shape.

A few minutes later, I felt an urge in my lower bowels and was able to complete what was unattainable a couple of days earlier. Relief flowed through me and my pants fit again. But, like turning 180 degrees, the following few days made constipation a desirable option. It started that night after I'd gone to bed. I felt the pressure begin to build in my lower abdomen.

For some bizarre reason (maybe it was the drugs), I was reminded of the times we baked homemade bread. Slowly the dough rose over the top of the bread pan and continued to grow. It felt like I had brewer's yeast gurgling and bubbling in my bowels.

My distended stomach began to hurt as I lay between the sheets. My sphincter muscle tightened and I gritted my teeth, but I knew the fight would be lost. The pressure was enormous. Suddenly, like a volcano, with many millennia of pent-up pressure, my backside erupted into one of the loudest, crudest and vile-smelling explosions I had ever produced. Images of Mt. St. Helens invaded my brain.

And it felt so-o-o-o-o-o good!

Caroline told me in no uncertain terms, she could smell sulphur when she got to the top of the stairs, halfway across the house from our bedroom.

The wet face cloth over her mouth and nose did little for intimacy.

The condition abated over the following three or four days after each treatment.

About that time, normal bathroom activity resumed.

Another phenomenon also occurred.

I called them the HIC-BURPS, a term which is not found in

your Funk and Wagnell, Webster's or the internet.

Because of my hiatus hernia, I had taken burping to new heights over the previous twenty years. I could burp the national anthem and "Na, na, na, na, na, na, na, na, hey, hey, hey, goodbye".

It was not different after the fourth poke. I routinely got the hiccups, again because of the chemo and other assorted gas producers I was ingesting. Wedged in between the hiccups, was the odd burp. First a high shrill hiccup, HHIIICCCUUUPPP; immediately followed by a gut-wrenching, BUURRRRPPP.

It was almost symphonic. I felt like a one-man walking percussion ensemble. In with the hiccup, out with the burp. It was a constant source of amusement for Chris and Jodi. It was embarrassing, however, when we were in public or doing our grocery shopping. I could've stopped traffic with the combination. Add the lower gas element and we're talking about an appearance on the Letterman show doing stupid, burp and fart tricks.

I often found myself laughing out loud at myself and the absurdity of it all. In the middle of my deadly serious fight against cancer, the comic relief was like ice cream on a steamy, hot summer day.

I didn't know whether to walk tight-assed or keep my mouth shut.

My family told me, both, preferably.

The down-from-the-bottom-of-the-stomach laughing and giggling was great therapy for all of us.

HHIIIIIICCCCCCCC---BBBBUUURRRRRRPPPPPP!!!!!!!!!

Excuse me!

Chapter 17

Journal entry: June 23. Had to sleep in the basement tonight because of the 40 degree heat. It rained just after supper making the air feel thick and muggy. I'm into my usual post treatment "funk" and I feel "blah". The pressure is welling up again in my fingertips and my feet are swollen and so hot. They seem to be retaining water. I hear my heart pounding more in my ears than usual. I'm going to get my blood pressure checked next time I'm in the clinic. We bought a big fan today to help us cool off.

WE'D BEEN WARNED THE Prednizone might create a bizarre side effect. It was as if Silly Putty was injected under the surface of the skin in my body. Whenever I removed my sneakers or sandals, I saw a hard, definite outline of where they'd produced pressure points on my feet. The indentures were still visible an hour after I'd removed the footwear. Drug-free normal feet would quickly have the markings fade away.

Sometimes my fingers and toes looked like uncooked sausages. When I made a fist, the knuckles and joints turned completely white, like they were devoid of any blood.

If I pressed a quarter into the skin on my forearm and held it for fifteen or twenty seconds, I'd almost be able to read the year the coin was minted.

And as usual, my mouth sores worsened, sometimes affecting the back of my throat, causing me difficulty in swallowing. A tightness could be felt at the base of my neck just under the Adam's apple and I suffered from constant hic-burps. All symptoms repeated themselves after each treatment. As much as I expected them to occur, it still was frustrating to deal with.

Another factor in my discomfort was the oppressive mid-summer scorching heat of daily plus 35 degree temperatures that intensified the swelling and numbness in my fingers and toes.

We bought a large fan and placed it by our open bedroom window at night in hopes of cooling things down. As it oscillated, it swirled the hot air around the stifling room. I began to understand the principles of a convection oven. We found ourselves sleeping in the basement more often where the relief of ten degree cooler temperatures made sleeping barely comfortable. Again and again, the warning of those in oncology echoed in my head, *get plenty of rest.*

We could barely afford the fan. Central air conditioning was a future luxury. I thought about filling our waterbed with ice cubes. In those uncomfortable, sticky, sleepless nights and not being able to sleep, I often turned on my bedside lamp and picked up my journal.

> *Journal entry: June 25 (2 a.m.) As I look*
> *back over the past four months, a multitude*
> *of thoughts criss-cross my mind. Am I – no*
> *– WILL I be the same person when this is*
> *finished? I don't see how I can be. Everything*
> *I experienced is no longer relevant. The same,*
> *small inconveniences that used to bother me*
> *will not factor into anything I do in the future.*
> *I hope I'm on a journey to rebirth, walking*
> *a new path that will undoubtedly take me to*
> *new adventures. The old trail is behind me.*

I've spent way too much time fretting about the future. Would I have changed anything if I knew the future was what I'm experiencing now? Probably. It's funny how, when a future might be taken away, it puts a whole new perspective on what life and living is really all about. I've always worked hard. I should laugh and play harder. I must see more humor in all I do, especially in light of the chemotherapy. That will be my immediate challenge. Laugh more. For the time being, I will keep a stiff upper lip, with a smattering of Mylanta on the dozen remaining mustache hairs because of my upset stomach. I'm sitting up in bed, propped by four pillows to keep the contents of my stomach out of my throat. My head is at the top of the headboard; my butt pushed to the bottom of the waterbed bladder. My stomach sounds like a bilge pump in high gear and my entire gastric tract has come alive. The antacids are engaging in hand-to-hand combat with the stomach contents. Just before she dozed off, Caroline said "have a good sleep". Sometimes she's a real riot.

Journal entry: June 27. Time for my second treatment in the fourth cycle. Had the poke at noon; felt fine and had supper at five. Hey! I'm on the downhill side of the treatments – just about half-way done. I'm going to the radio station to see if I can do any part-time on-air work to try to earn some extra money. The pittance I will get from U.I. doesn't cover the mortgage payments. God, how I hated going to the welfare office.

I received my first cheque from Unemployment Insurance.

I did not like to open the envelope but we desperately needed the money. I had to console myself with the thought that I'd worked for 24 years and had never tapped into the welfare system before.

But I still hated it. I had no choice, but to swallow my pride. I had to do it for my family and I swore I'd make it up in spades when I was back working. Early that morning, unable to sleep again, I wrote:

> *Journal entry: June 28. (1:40 a.m.) It's a vicious circle. When I'm not feeling well and sleep does not come easily, it's simple to take a tranquilizer and then nod off. But it's not a natural sleep and the next day, I suffer through a drug hangover – and do not feel any better than if I hadn't slept at all. I suffer from irregular sleep patterns and often wake up at 2 or 3 in the morning, like this morning, and never really get back to a sound sleep again. Then I try to play catch-up all day long. I'm so frustrated at having to live within these narrow parameters. I once had the freedom to do and be as I wished and took it for granted. Now, I'm restricted in everything I do, think or act because I don't have control over my body and in my body and what's happening to it. I have to force myself to eat, to sleep – and to do so with the help of chemicals. I think I know what a toxic waste site is. At the same time, I have to force myself to concentrate on not being stressed – which is a stress in itself. It's very much like being an inmate, only in this case, an inmate living in a prison without walls. Are these walls being erected by me? Why is it in the beautiful Okanagan Valley on a crystal clear blue day I'm watching the cherries on our neighbor's tree turning red while sequestered*

inside the kitchen. The truth is, I'm confined within myself. No locks. No chains. No heavy steel doors. It's now almost 2 o'clock. My eyes are so very sore, the kind of sore you feel from crying too much. I want so much to sleep soundly, naturally, without popping pills. But there are so many nerve endings still alive and energized, refusing to follow the dictates of my mind. They're much more than alive – they're dancing just under my skin. Where did I leave my container of pills?

Journal entry: June 28 (10 p.m.) My cousin, her husband and children arrived from Germany this afternoon about 4. I did not feel well and would rather have been alone but I put on a brave face because we'd never met them before. They know about my Hodgkin's. But I must challenge myself to put aside how I feel to accommodate them.

Having never re-visited my German birthplace, I spent a lot of time asking them about the old country. Caroline and I had talked about visiting my family over the years.

My cousin commented on the beauty of the valley and particularly how the drive to Naramata reminded her of Italy and Germany. She told us the climates were nearly identical and was impressed how the orchards and vineyards looked like her homeland.

Two days later they left to visit my brothers and sisters in other parts of British Columbia and Alberta.

As June ended, the cherries ripened. Being first-year Okanaganites, we decided to preserve fruit. On the last week-end of the month, we hand picked some of the cherries and apricots from a local orchardist, bought a cherry pit remover and dug out two dozen dusty jars from the basement. My task for the canning effort was to operate the cherry pit remover and I discovered I had a lot of difficulty operating the small device because of the numbness in my fingertips. I struggled through six ice cream pails of cherries.

We spent that Sunday in the summer heat, over a stove, canning and then stocking the shelves in our cold room with jars of fruit. We'd been told by others the insane impulse to preserve everything in sight is acted upon only by those who initially move to the valley. The desire, we were also informed, wanes with each passing year.

> *Journal entry: July 6. I find the weakness in my limbs very tough to take. Even though my weight is about 155 pounds, I'm weaker. I still, however try to stay active. We biked the entire two-and-a-half mile length of the channel pathway this evening.*
>
> *(12:52 a.m.) Back on the toilet again. My stomach is kicking back hard.*

The bike ride we took along the pathway adjacent to the channel that connects Skaha and Okanagan Lakes was the last one of the summer. The abject weakness was staggering and the fear of falling off the bicycle and injuring myself weighed heavily in my decision. I found I had to concentrate just to walk. I tripped over uneven cracks in the sidewalk because my feet were dragging. I had to amble in a wider stance to keep from tipping over. It felt weird and my awkward gait must've looked almost comical to others.

In this grim reality, I wasn't laughing much.

Grocery shopping became a chore. Items I could've easily picked up in the past with my fingertips, like a jar of pickles or a large pop took the effort of both hands. I spent most of my time behind the grocery cart, holding onto it like an elderly person would a walker, my feet shuffling down the aisles.

I could no longer walk upstairs in our house without using

the hand railing. I could only take one step at a time and my breathing was heavy when I got to the top, at the fourteenth step. *Don't be a wimp*, I screamed at myself. *Take two at a time, like you always do. You're a jam tart! DO IT!*

My legs could not respond.

I abandoned all hopes of pouring the concrete pad and finishing the work on the carport. We didn't have the money and I had no strength left. I gave in to the reality that I would not be able to complete the plans I had so carefully laid out only a few months earlier.

In mid-July, my brother and his family drove from Salmon Arm to spend a Sunday at the beach with us. They joined our family in the sun – except for me. We had chosen a portion of Skaha Beach where several large trees cast shadows on the sand underneath. There I sat, an avid sunbather, in the shade. I wore a long-sleeve shirt, cotton sweatpants and my goofy looking straw hat on my head, slathered in 30 SPF sunscreen on what little exposed skin was showing.

Before the chemotherapy, I tanned well and often fell asleep, face up in the sun.

In envy, I looked around at the bronzed bodies. The smell of cocoa butter was delicious as it wafted up from the water. Life around me was in constant, swirling motion. Parents were laughing and kids screaming. Rollerbladers zipped by on the concrete walkway behind us. In the distance, on the asphalt courts, young men and women were shooting baskets, while several games of beach volleyball were going on behind them.

I turned back to the lake in front of us. Swimmers by the hundreds frolicked in the warm water. Flotillas of boaters and people on personal watercrafts created a small surf that broke onto the sand a hundred feet away. In a whirling kaleidoscope of color and sound, the world passed me by. I was relegated to being an observer and no longer an active participant in life.

My days were often spent in front of the TV, with the sounds of traffic coming through the screen door. Because Penticton is a summer vacation destination for many Canadians and Americans, the bustle of vehicular activity on the streets often carried on long after midnight. I lay in bed and frequently heard the throaty rumble of a high performance car as it broke the stillness of the early morning, the tires chirping as the driver shifted gears. The car roared down the street behind our house, the engine still winding up. I wished I was doing the shifting.

> *Journal entry: July 18. Four months down, four*
> *to go. I'm halfway through my chemotherapy.*
> *My moustache is just about gone again. My*
> *hair, which comes back a bit between treatments*
> *is falling out again. Started my fifth cycle today.*
> *I'm into a rhythm, knowing what to expect. We*
> *received some shocking news today. A phone call*
> *that Jeff Dejong, the son of friends of ours was*
> *diagnosed with lung cancer. What a jolt! I will*
> *talk with him when I return to Lethbridge in a*
> *couple of days to pick up our antique car.*

When we heard Jeff had been diagnosed, it stunned all of us. We'd known his parents Joyce and Pete for 15 years. They were our neighbors in Lethbridge and we'd seen Jeff, his brother Craig and sister Trish grow up with our kids.

Our hearts poured out for him. I gritted my teeth and vowed not to let the news set me back physically or emotionally. Occasionally I'd heard of celebrities in the news who'd been diagnosed with cancer succumb to the disease. It was tough not to let it affect me.

This isn't fair, I wrote. *It wasn't fair when it happened to me and it's certainly not fair that Jeff is facing cancer. I'm halfway through my life. Jeff's only 22.*

Chapter 18

THREE DAYS AFTER STARTING my fifth cycle in July, Jodi and I climbed into our old truck at 7 a.m. for our trip back to Lethbridge. I really didn't want to go but we had to make the journey. Months before our move to Penticton, she'd planned a weeklong camping trip to Waterton Park on the Alberta-Montana border with some friends. On my way back home I would stop at the Annable's to bring back our antique car.

Two weeks earlier, the Garnet fire had erupted, blanketing the south Okanagan in thick, choking smoke. Coupled with temperatures in the high 30's, it made breathing difficult for me. I eagerly anticipated getting a reprieve from the polluted air.

By the time we reached Salmon Arm, the air was clean and we no longer smelled smoke. I headed to Wolf's house to borrow his tandem axle car trailer on which I would bring back our classic. Once we were hooked up, we headed east on the Trans Canada to southern Alberta.

For 400 miles, the hot summer sun sent the temperatures to around 35 degrees.

Near Jaffray, just west of the BC-Alberta border, Jodi and I stopped in a clearing off the highway to the right, got out and climbed into the back of the pickup. Under the tall cedars in the shade, each of us sitting on a fender well, we ate cold chicken and drank ice water from our cooler. It was one of the most memorable meals I can remember.

We opened the rear slider of the cab and listened to the rock songs. It felt so good, in spite of the tribulation in our lives, to be alive, to be chatting with my daughter about the music of the Beatles, our favorite band.

We arrived in Lethbridge about 7 that night and I dropped Jodi off at her friend's house. Arrangements had been made for her to be brought home a week later. I took a side trip to visit Jeff Dejong in Coaldale, six miles east of the city. His hair had started falling out and he looked tired. I gave him a big hug and commented about his hair loss and told him, "been there, doing that". I encouraged him to fight and be positive and shared with him the concepts of visualization and positive thinking. I also challenged him to stay as fit as possible. I said goodbye and headed north an hour-and-a-half to the Annable farm in Carmangay where I would spend the night. I arrived about 10 and I sat up till midnight reminiscing with Colleen and Lloyd and like the previous trip, didn't get much sleep.

Next morning after breakfast, we loaded and chained up the old muscle car on the trailer and I headed back into the mountains through Calgary. The prairie temperatures were pleasant, in the mid 20's as I left the Stampede city behind me and rolled west through Banff and Lake Louise. I put my cassette of upbeat Roy Orbison tunes into the tape deck and tapped along to the music with my fat fingers on the steering wheel.

Near Golden, about halfway home, the mercury had sky-rocketed. Because I was towing 5,000 pounds of antique auto and trailer up and down mountain highways, including the rarified air at the Rogers Pass, my eyes were glued to the temperature gauge in the dashboard. At Golden, it read 230 degrees. *Just right for poaching eggs*, I thought.

I turned in at the A&W, parked the unit and turned off the big block 402 engine. I opened the hood and the blast of heat almost knocked me backwards. In a quick, visual inspection, everything appeared to be okay – until my eyes fell on the fuel filter, in the small rubber hose at the front of the carburetor. They widened in disbelief. The gasoline was bubbling inside the clear plastic housing.

"The bloody stuff is boiling", I muttered aloud to myself and then thought, *I think I should step back very quickly*. I left the hood up to help the heat escape, bought lunch and ate it on an outside table, some distance away from the truck.

If it blows up, at least I'll have a ring-side seat.

Half-an-hour later, I checked all the fluid levels. The coolant was down significantly so I borrowed a plastic jug full of water from one of the servers at the restaurant, filled the radiator, closed the hood and returned the container.

With one eye on the road and the other on the heat gauge, I arrived back home late that night. The smoke from the forest fire was still lingering, thick and heavy. With the springs in the old truck and the joints in my body creaking, I slowly slid out of the cab and opened the front door, kissed Caroline 'hello' and fell into bed.

> *Journal entry: Sunday July 31. Chris turned 18 today. We had a small party for him and his cousin Jonathan who had just turned four. It's still really hot. After cake and ice cream we went to Skaha Beach and walked in the water at the shore. Every time I do that, it feels so good on my aching feet.*

My sister Carolyn, husband Mike, daughter Meagan and son Jonathan had joined us for a couple of days earlier from Calgary for a vacation in the valley. As I watched Chris accept his gifts, I was so thankful that I was alive to be with him at his eighteenth birthday.

As August slowly slipped by, we experienced one of the hottest summers in recent memory, according to a lot of the long time residents. We suffered through six weeks of temperatures in the high 30's to low 40's. With the forest fires finally contained near the end of the month, I prepared myself for my seventh treatment.

Carol and Rome stayed with us for a couple of days after returning from completing the physically strenuous West Coast Trail adventure on Vancouver Island.

They told us of the six days of wilderness hiking with no amenities.

I countered with, "What? No fast food, fried chicken or keys for the bathroom? No showers for a week? Not for me thank you. I don't need anything else to make me smell bad."

They'd also timed their excursion to watch the Ironman Canada Triathlon held in Penticton on the last Sunday of August each year. Triathletes from around the globe had converged on the city to participate in one of the most grueling sporting events known to humanity.

The Ironman starts at 7 a.m. and consists of three events: a 2.4 mile swim, a 112 mile bike course and finishes with a full 26.2 mile marathon for a total of 140.6 miles.

The 40 or 50 professionals who compete for money and status complete the triathlon in eight to nine hours. Most people however, simply try to get to the finish line before the cutoff time at midnight to earn a finisher's medal and T-shirt.

I never knew much about Ironman when we lived in Lethbridge and didn't even know it was held in Penticton each summer.

On the morning of the race, the four of us arrived at the swim venue about 6:30 and joined the thousands of spectators lined up behind a temporary five foot high fence along the edge of the beach about two hundred feet from the swim start. I couldn't believe my eyes. The sea of triathletes in their black wetsuits and yellow swim caps, waited for the start of the race.

At 7 sharp, the cannon heralded the start of the 1994

Ironman. 1,700 bodies hit the water, 6,800 arms and legs flailed in the boiling sea of humanity. They were heading to the large, white houseboat a mile away, in the first leg of the swim.

As I watched the scene unfold before me, a sudden, unexplainable feeling washed over me like a tidal wave. I realized that somehow, someway, the sensation I felt that morning was to have enormous consequences that would change the direction of the rest of my life.

I ached to be out there in the middle of the teeming horde, even though I'd never learned to swim. Memories of working out in the weight room, cycling and playing hockey flooded into my mind. I gazed down at my flabby stomach and spindly legs that didn't allow me to walk for more than 10 minutes without having to stop and rest.

I looked up again at the scene in the water a half a football field away in front of me. Tears welled up and the picture blurred into a haze of motion, colors and sounds. I leaned over to Caroline, my voice quivering and choking and blurted out something that seemed to come from someplace and somebody else and from somewhere that I had no control over.

"I'm going to do this someday".

The second that statement left my lips, it seemed to be like a ray of hope and affirmation for the future. On that gorgeous Sunday morning, my metamorphosis, my rebirth into a new future, had begun. It could well have been the most single, important moment in my life.

And I didn't know it at the time.

> *Journal entry: September 7. I'm not getting the euphoric highs as I did in the past but it doesn't matter anymore. Even though there are many somber moments because of the compounding effects of the chemo, I cannot get that moment out of my mind. Like a Polaroid, that instantaneous moment is burned into my memory forever. It is the beacon in the darkness.*

It guides me, inspires me, gives me yet another
reason to fight on. It still get the feelings of
horror about this disease and sometimes they
sneak past the armor of hope I've fortified myself
with. It's difficult at times to stay focused and
positive But I will consistently make room for
optimism and hope. "Ironman" I love the sound
of the word.

I began my seventh cycle on the day after Jodi's birthday on September 15th.

Seven days later, I was one month away from completing my 32-week sentence of chemotherapy.

And for the first time in months, on September 18th, I excitedly went back to work. I was asked to do a radio broadcast from a local sports store and it felt great to be back on the air again. I was pumped with excitement and no sweats to chatter through.

The owners of the store were Janelle and Lyle Biagioni. I got to know her as the remote began and found out we both had interesting stories to share. She'd just finished writing a book about how her first husband, an RCMP officer, had been injured in a motorcycle accident and succumbed to his injuries a few months later.

Janelle recommended I publish my journal writings. She was a founding member of the Penticton Writers and Publishers; a group of four women with a love of writing who were helping others do the same. I was thankful I'd put my thoughts over the previous seven months on paper and tried to imagine what it would be like to write a book.

Journal entry: September 20. This is where
the surrealism kicks in. What happened in the
last seven months is now history. Where did
all those eternity-long minutes and hours go?
The ones in which I was trapped when time

stood still. In my VCR of life they are stored,
only to be replayed and re-lived when I read
them. I have learned much, the most important
being that life is so very, absolutely precious. I
don't want to waste anymore time just 'being'.
I want to really explore and experience life to
the fullest and to give more of myself to me and
those I love. I will explore all of my creativity
that I've put on the back burner in the last
couple of decades. Maybe I will write a book,
start painting again like I used to. I'd love to
learn to play a piano or the old guitar Caroline
gave me so long ago that I've never picked up.
What's holding me back? ME – that's who! I
can use my illness as a springboard to live and
love, to explore and play. I think, however, I
should not 'think' about things so much. I will
lose precious time when I should be 'doing'
stuff instead. I know one thing for sure. Before
I do anything, I'm going to get back into shape
again, physically -better than I've ever been. It's
going to feel so good again to hurt in a positive
manner while I rebuild my soft, useless muscles.

A miracle happened on September 21ˢᵗ. We received a $1,900 income tax refund cheque from Revenue Canada. We'd been in a dispute over that total for two years and an adjudicator had ruled in our favor. It couldn't have come at a better time because my U.I. had run out and we'd already started cashing in our RRSP's. It was like a windfall from heaven when that letter arrived. Also in the mail was my C.R.A. diploma. We framed it and hung it in the family room and celebrated the achievement.

Over the following few weeks I did more radio remotes and it helped to mask the feelings of weariness that had enveloped me. My mind, body and soul were worn out because of the ups, the downs, the doubts and celebrations. I was physically, mentally and spiritually exhausted, yet through the emotional turmoil, I prepared myself for the last cycle of chemotherapy.

> *Journal entry: October 1. Hard to believe.*
> *October is here already. One more monthly*
> *chemo session – two more pokes.*

Just two more treatments. I couldn't believe it. I looked in the mirror that morning and through the droopy eyelids staring back, saw a faint smile form at the corners of my mouth.

Chapter 19

Journal entry: October 11. Here it is! The beginning of the end. I get poke 15 this afternoon, I'm pleased to be holding my weight at about 157. But from here on in, I'm not going to force-feed myself anymore. I'll wait and see how my hunger will be affected by the radiation. My face is flushed and I feel the usual stomach discomfort. I have to temper my desire to have this all come to an end right now. I'm so tired of it all. I want to be finished <u>right now.</u> I don't want to do the final chemo and I'm certainly not anxious to spend four weeks in Vancouver. I've heard some real unpleasant things about radiation.

I DON'T REMEMBER HOW often in my life I'd used the term, 'sick and tired'. I felt like I'd been battling an eight month bout with the flu. I'd experienced all the possible emotions a human being could face.

I was truly exhausted and didn't know how much more I could have endured. I wanted to call it quits; to scream out at the top of my lungs for the whole world to hear:

NO MORE! THAT'S IT! I'M NOT GOING THROUGH ANOTHER TREATMENT!

I SIMPLY CANNOT TAKE IT ANYMORE!

But, I knew I wouldn't quit. I would go through the final treatments for my family, friends and me. I received a call from oncology and was told I had an appointment with a cancer specialist at Vancouver General Hospital on October 25th, one week after my final poke. Caroline had booked a week off work so we could be together for the few days it took to get prepared for radiation therapy. I didn't like the thought of being away for a whole month.

On the evening of October 14th, the phone rang and I answered it. The man calling represented the 1995 BC Summer Games Committee. He said he was very sorry to tell me my application for Games Coordinator had been lost in the mail. He received it three weeks after the cut-off date. He said he was impressed with my qualifications and apologized again. My chance at a $30,000 job evaporated.

Thirty thousand dollars. For us, it would have been like winning a lottery.

I was speechless, then angry, but I knew I had to let it go. I tried not to think about it, but the thought of losing the opportunity sat in my stomach like sulfuric acid for a couple of days. It was difficult not to blame anyone.

I fought to remain positive, typed out a new resume and began searching the want-ads. There were no full time opportunities at any of the radio stations in the valley. I knew I had to take the initiative and find work. A job would not come knocking at our front door.

Journal entry. October 17. I'm being tugged by several emotions tonight. Firstly, I'm so glad the final chemo is tomorrow. Secondly, I must keep my emotions in check because there is still a long road of healing ahead of me. Thirdly, how can I be sure the cancer is gone? This thought constantly nags at me as I get closer to the final poke. The fear comes from the deepest, darkest corner of my mind. I just can't fathom going through this again. The thought makes my skin crawl.

Journal entry: October 18. Final poke today. It's over. IT'S FINALLY ALL OVER!

When I walked into the clinic at noon for my final treatment, I was overwhelmed with the feelings which had compounded themselves over the previous 32 weeks. For the first time since that fateful first poke, the lump in my throat was not because of the chemotherapy.

All of the oncology nurses had been so supportive. They'd become friends and soul mates. I'd poured out my thoughts and feelings to them and when the blackness of despair seemed to overtake my positive attitude, they listened and dialogued with genuine interest. I often thought about them. It had to be extremely difficult administering treatments to some patients who had no hope, no future. What was it like to look into the eyes of a woman or man who would not be alive in three, six, or maybe nine months.

How did they deal with that? I wondered if the caregivers broke down when they arrived home, sometimes after a very trying day. It knew it was not just a 'job' for them.

Tanis Colletti administered my final poke. Jodi was there to take a couple of pictures. I hugged each of the nurses when the treatment was concluded; Christine, Claire, Vivian Hudon, Shirley Fladager, Tanis and Jack. I took a moment with him, put both my hands on his shoulders, looked him squarely in the eyes and told him how very grateful I was for his gift of healing, his compassion, his empathy and friendship.

He then reciprocated my hug.

At our evening supper we talked about our trip to the coast. Caroline would drive home a few days after I was settled in at the Cancer Lodge, a facility operated by the Canadian Cancer Society.

That night as we snuggled in bed, she cried and I held her

tightly. We tried to sleep, but it was elusive. She asked how she could leave me there for a month. I told her I'd be back by bus for a weekend halfway through the radiation that I'd receive once a day, Mondays through Fridays.

Two days later, I got home at suppertime after a couple of media job interviews in Kelowna. As we ate, I expressed my hope for getting a position quickly. Caroline cautioned me about being too anxious to get back to work.

I told her again, how much I hated being on Unemployment Insurance and would do anything to get off the dole. My medical U.I. was discontinued after fifteen weeks and I'd applied for assistance a couple of weeks earlier and was placed in the general stream of those looking for work.

If I have to pump gas, I'll do it, I promised myself.

We left for Vancouver at 6 p.m. October 24th. It rained most of the way and at the higher elevation of Manning Park we drove through 20 miles of wet, heavy snow. Five hours later, we arrived at the Easter Seal House. It's a clean, simple facility for families of those undergoing treatments for a variety of illnesses to live for a temporary period of time.

The following morning, at Vancouver General, I was examined by a phalanx of cancer specialists. They prodded and poked me with a variety of instruments and I was X-rayed again. An hour later, I met with the last oncologist, Dr. Randall Fairey. Caroline and I had been waiting in the examination room when he walked in. He introduced himself to us and then looked down at the information on his clipboard. He was silent as he scanned and flipped the papers.

I sensed that something was not quite what it should be. *What's going on?* I looked at Caroline and saw she'd suddenly become worried. It seemed like several minutes had ticked by when Dr. Fairey said something that made us sit up.

"I don't know if you'll need the radiation treatments."

We couldn't believe what he'd just said.

"Pardon?"

"Well, according to your X-rays and tests, there is virtually no evidence of any active cancer. There are a couple of what we call, 'hot spots' just behind your lungs where the large tumors were. But they may simply be scar tissue that is healing."

Caroline and I looked at each other in wild disbelief. All the planning, the uncertainty, the worrying we'd gone through since the end of my treatments had us feeling very apprehensive about the radiation and the side effects.

"Does this mean we get to go home?" she blurted out.

"There really is no need for you to stay here any longer", he nodded. "However, this doesn't mean you won't need radiation," he said, throwing caution on our joy. "I'm still going to go ahead and book the treatments as we had originally planned."

Claire had already arranged the four weeks of radiation to start at the end of October. Dr. Fairey told us he would get hold of Jack with the results of his findings the following day and they'd discuss the next course of action.

Just before we left, Dr. Fairey told us Caroline and I would be involved in any decision making and added, "your chance of cure is about 70 percent without radiation. With the therapy, it's only slightly higher," and again detailed the harshness of the treatments.

I especially didn't like the part about not being able to wash or use underarm deodorant in the area to be radiated and because lymph nodes are found in the armpits, I couldn't use my Mennen for a month. The thought of it made me gag.

He continued, "radiation could also cause extreme fatigue and upset stomach, and like chemotherapy, it can also destroy good tissue as well as that which is cancerous". He also explained that once the therapy is used to treat a specific part of the body, it's not usually performed again in the same area.

"If there's a recurrence of your cancer in the future, we can then look at this treatment as a back-up procedure. In the meantime, you might as well head home and I'll call Jack. He'll want to talk to you tomorrow."

We shook Dr. Fairey's hand vigorously and thanked him profusely, then bounded out of the hospital like a couple of kids. Thirty minutes later, about 4:30, we'd checked out of the Easter Seal House and were on our way back to Penticton, creeping through the typical, heavy Vancouver afternoon drive home traffic.

We still couldn't believe what had just happened. It seemed too good to be true.

Could the chemotherapy have destroyed all the cancer cells? Was it unusual? Don't the majority of lymphoma patients require radiation?

All of a sudden we had a flurry of questions. We'd been too excited to ask them at the time when Dr. Fairey gave us the news.

Time flew by as we hurried home as quickly as possible. Our minds still spinning, we drove up in front of our house around 9:30.

"What are you guys doing home?" the kids asked as we shot through the front door and told them the exciting news.

The following morning we heard from the Vancouver clinic. My radiation date had been rescheduled to begin November 14th. We met with Jack on October 27th, in the same office where eight months earlier, my chemotherapy odyssey had begun. He'd studied the reports from Dr. Fairey and those of his associates. Caroline and I were holding hands as we sat across from Jack. He was smiling and seemed quite relaxed, a far cry from my first meeting with him. In his hand was his ever-present clipboard. We chatted for a few moments. He looked at his notes and then presented us with two options.

We do radiation.

We don't do radiation.

He mentioned the 70 percent chance of being cured, the same number given us by Dr. Fairey. "How does that sit with you?" Jack asked. We both said 80 or 90 percent or more would be better if we were given a choice. He smiled sympathetically and said he couldn't give us those numbers.

I'd never been asked for input into a decision that could determine the amount of time I had left on this earth. I felt clammy. I was hot and cold at the same time. It was like re-visiting a night sweat. Caroline gripped my hand so tight, her knuckles turned white.

"We're not gamblers," she said quietly. "Isn't this like gambling with Wally's life?" I reached over and handed her a tissue from the box on Jack's desk.

"I don't look at this as taking an unnecessary risk by not submitting to radiation," our friend told us. "Dr. Fairey is one of the best and I concur with him that the radiotherapy is not always automatically prescribed and may not have to be undertaken in your case".

The three of us discussed our options for a half hour, then came to a conclusion, with Dr. Chritchley spelling out the course of action. He said he would cancel the radiation and instead, have me undergo two Gallium Scans, thirty days apart. He explained the procedure uses nuclear medicine to identify hot spots after cancer treatments.

Jack went on to say, "if the spots behind your lungs have diminished or better yet, are non-existent four weeks after the first scan, there will be no more treatment".

We rarely bought 649 tickets. That afternoon we took the biggest gamble in our lives. After supper that night, the four of us held hands and Caroline and I assured the kids we had made the right decision.

> *Journal entry: Friday October 28. What a day!*
> *Five hundred miles to Vancouver and back for a*
> *single shot of nuclear medicine. Drove home in*
> *some wicked winter conditions at the mountain*
> *passes. I get to do it all over again on Monday*
> *morning for the scan. I can hardly wait.*

I left for the coast at 7:00 that Friday morning and just after noon was injected with the Gallium at the Heather Clinic at Vancouver General and a half hour later, was on my way back home. The technician who gave me the shot said the drug would take 72 hours to totally infiltrate my body. Three days later, I would have the first of two X-rays to highlight any possible cancer.

Early Monday morning I headed west again to Vancouver dressed comfortably in my sweat pants, top and sneakers. At noon, in a large examining room, a technician asked me to lie on a straight, narrow, cloth covered, foam insulated table. There were several other hospital-type cubical stalls in the vicinity, with curtains on overhead rails, that could be opened and closed.

She pulled the curtain around me, put a pillow under my head and knees, tucked my arms snuggly to my body and suggested I relax because the first half of the procedure would take about thirty minutes. She brought my attention to the camera above me that would inch very slowly along an overhead track from my head to toes, taking incremental X-rays of the length of my body. I flashed back to the lymphangiogram. *But hey, this isn't too bad* I thought. *No needles, no blood, no black goop to be blasted between my toes.* She turned on the camera and I heard a soft noise as it began its journey to my feet. I began to doze off as the lens came into sight above me, barely an inch from my nose.

A half-hour later, she woke me up and asked me to move to a different table with another camera, which would take 360 degree pictures along my torso from my shoulders to my hips as the camera revolved around me. The narrow table seemed to have less padding than the previous one. She asked me to place my hands straight above my head and to fold my fingers. I told her I had bursitis in my left shoulder and that I'd separated both of them several times over the years playing hockey. She took some soft binding and loosely tied my elbows together.

"Sorry", she said, "but we have to do it this way to fully expose your chest cavity to get a proper reading of your lungs and the hot spots." I winced from the small stabs of pain as I brought my arms up as she requested.

"This will take about 45 minutes", she informed me. "To get accurate pictures, you have to lie absolutely still". She pulled the camera, with a two-square foot lens jutting from it, just below my chin and switched it on. It sounded louder than the first one as I saw it move slowly to my right. Like the sun sets in the west, it disappeared out of my peripheral sight in a couple of minutes. The radiologists would be able to look at the pictures in 3-D fashion.

As the unit dropped away, I again tried to take myself away via daydreams. The discomfort in my shoulders slowly turned to pain, then numbness. I unlocked my fingers and curled and straightened them a bit without moving my arms. I also wiggled my hips as little as possible knowing the camera was recording only the conditions in my chest. I tightened and relaxed the muscles in my butt to keep the circulation flowing.

Be great for the buns of steel video wouldn't it?

As the minutes painstakingly ticked away, my shoulders, hips, and heels all turned to stone. I fought back the feelings to sit up and massage some life back into the numb parts of my anatomy.

Forty-five minutes later, the camera stopped at my mid-section and I heard a series of beeps. *Just like my microwave – and man, am I done!*

The technician moved the camera away from my body and untied the bindings.

My limp, useless left arm fell in a semi-circle over the edge of the table and dangled over the side. I screamed in pain which startled her. I gritted my teeth, reached across my body and pulled my lifeless limb by the sleeve of the sweatshirt and cradled it across my chest like a child would a doll.

"Are you okay?" she asked with a worried look.

I nodded and slowly sat up and gave myself a few minutes to get my arm limber again. Gradually, all feeling returned. Then the throbbing set in. I thanked her and slid off the examination table, still holding my arm.

What the hell am I thanking her for, I wondered.

I walked to Dr. Fairey's office two hours later and waited for our appointment to get his reading on the Gallium Scan. He grinned as he walked into the room and told me he did see two small spots in the middle of my chest which were once tennis ball sized growths almost a year earlier.

"I suspect it might be the scar tissue I talked about when we last met. The next scan will be much more enlightening". I pumped his hand in farewell and told him I'd be back in a month.

I was becoming very familiar with the Trans Canada Highway to Hope and for the third time in four weeks, I was heading back east in heavy traffic.

In the interim, between the tests, I was elected President of the Penticton Unit of the Canadian Cancer Society. The annual general meeting of the BC/Yukon Division was scheduled for the first weekend in Richmond, near Vancouver. As Unit President, I was entitled to attend the conference. Luckily, it coincided with the date of my follow-up Gallium Scan.

Ralph Robinson gave me an airline voucher for the flight when I mentioned the rough winter driving conditions on Highway 3 to him after doing some commercials at the station. I do not fly well, but I decided to take a break from fighting the snow and ice in our car and gratefully accepted the gift.

Two days before my Friday departure for the conference in early December, I did a very stupid thing. I watched the movie 'Alive'. It's the true story about a plane that went down in a blizzard in the Andes Mountains in 1972. Many members of a South American soccer team survived for two-and-a-half months on a mountaintop by eating the frozen flesh of those who perished in the crash.

The morning of departure, I picked up four Valium tablets, as prescribed by Dr. Harries, at my pharmacy. That evening I took two of the pills 45 minutes before take-off about 6. I was hoping I'd be winged away in a Dash-8, a two engine turbo prop plane that can carry almost 50 passengers. I'd flown in them before and the larger size of the aircraft made me feel quite safe. That was not the case that evening.

Instead, the four of us flying to Vancouver were directed to a small 19 seat aircraft. It was snowing slightly with the temperature around freezing. *This thing is no bigger than a bird*, I said to myself as I walked up the three steps into the tiny fuselage with the other passengers. We were greeted by a perky attendant with a wide smile who welcomed us aboard.

Bet her smile would be gone if she saw 'Alive'.

Thankfully the pills had kicked in at that time and I was enveloped in a velvet mellow fog. I had my Walkman and a couple of tapes of my favorite rock and roll. I put the volume to 'maximum'. *If I'm going down in flames, I didn't want to hear the screams of the others.* I looked around me and decided that was dumb.

I don't like to sit in window seats but when there is only one row of seats on each side of the aircraft there are no choices. *Geez, why didn't I get a Cheech and Chong movie, or something else with a really significant social meaning.* I hit the start button on my tape. "....born to be wiiillllllld..." reverberated in the fuzz which had replaced my brain.

To my surprise, the flight went so smoothly, the fifty minute trip was over before I knew it. I got off the plane and on wobbly legs made my way to the airport entrance where I was to be picked up by a Mason's driver. They offered free rides for cancer patients to and from the Vancouver Airport. I introduced myself to the man who was standing by the marked Mason's station wagon and asked to be taken to the hotel in Richmond where the conference was taking place.

Over the following three days, I met with many cancer patients, most in remission, and some, like myself, who'd just finished their chemotherapy or radiation treatments – or both. Hundreds of executives and volunteers from BC and the Yukon were also in attendance.

I said my good-byes on Sunday afternoon and got a ride from another Mason to the Canadian Cancer Society's Lodge near VGH where I was booked for the night. Like many across Canada, they are comfortable hotel-type buildings with a laid-back ambiance. The cost is nominal with good meals provided. Each room had two beds, desks and drawers. I met many wonderful men and women in various stages of treatment.

The following morning, Monday, December 5th, I was back at the Heather Pavilion for my second Gallium Scan. Knowing what to expect, I carefully limbered up my sore shoulder for ten minutes and asked to have the second part of the examination, first. It wasn't quite as painful as the initial test a month prior and I slept through the final portion of the procedure.

About three that afternoon, back at Dr. Fairey's office, I heard him say what I was praying he would, "there's no evidence of any active cancer. You go home and tell the good news to your family."

I gave him a bear hug, thanked him again and met with the Mason's driver at the parking lot for the drive back to the airport. The Valium tempered my excitement but I'm certain I could have outraced that plane back home. It touched down just after 7.

Caroline, Jodi and Chris were there in the middle of the activity at the Penticton Airport and we had a family hug and cry. Big, warm, wonderful tears of happiness.

When we got back home we decided we would go to Hawaii as soon as we could afford to. We deserved it. It would be our gift to ourselves for what we'd endured. It would be our payback.

Sleep was elusive that night, but I couldn't have cared less.

For the first time in more than eight months, I saw a bright, promise-filled future for me and those I loved.

The light at the end of the tunnel was a brilliant spotlight. I did see some darkness around the periphery, an uncertainty only time could erase.

I felt as if I were on the stage again – this time the star of my own show.

I DID HAVE A FUTURE! And it wasn't really important how long it would be.

What did matter, was what I would do with that future. I'd been given another chance to re-write the script for the rest of my life.

There was so much I wanted to do. A merry-go-round could not conjure up the color, sound and speed that flashed through my mind in vivid images of all I would and could do. I saw myself writing books, painting and drawing again, learning to play the guitar, restoring my 409 and vacationing in Hawaii, frolicking in the sand with my family.

Where's my hockey equipment

I could hardly wait to get that Victoriaville stick in my gloves again.

My heart was swelling with love and hope. As I lay beside Caroline, I looked at the clock. 4:22 a.m. Sometime shortly after that, in the early hours of that wintry morning, I finally drifted off to sleep.

Chapter 20

*Journal entry: December 6. First day back
on skates in over 2 years. I fell down. It's like
starting over again. I did manage finally to stay
up for 15 minutes but it felt much longer. The
muscle loss is horrible. I can't remember the last
time my legs felt so much like rubber.*

I ARRIVED AT THE McLaren Arena a few minutes after eight in
the evening, halfway through the Tuesday night family skate.
Wearing my dark blue sweatsuit and carrying my helmet,
hockey gloves and skates in my sports bag, I walked into the
lobby of the rink.

The butterflies in my stomach felt more like giant moths.

I couldn't believe how nervous I was. I'd become a stranger to my skates and I wasn't sure how my legs would respond
to being on the ice again after such a lengthy layoff. I sat on
one of the benches near the doors to the ice surface. Dozens
of kids and parents milled about during the break while the
Zamboni driver cleaned the ice. The noise was almost deafening and I felt the adrenaline in my body begin to flow. I took
off my sneakers and pried open my dusty, dried out size 7
Bauer's.

It was all I could do to hold the tongues open as I inserted
a foot in each. The numbness in my fingers didn't enable me
to get a solid grip, and they hurt when I tightened up the lac-

es. Beads of sweat formed on my forehead. I stopped to wipe it with a towel I had in the bag.

I took a deep breath, paused, then stood up. *I wish I had a stick in my hands. I need all the balance I can get.* I took an uncertain, wobbly step. I didn't want to fall down in front of the kids on the ice, so I decided to practice walking on the rubberized floor for a bit first. Having an eight year old laugh at me would not have done wonders for my confidence.

The monitor blew his whistle meaning the ice had been resurfaced. I waited till the hoard of youngsters stampeded by me to the rink entrance. When the tornado of miniature humanity was gone, I slowly walked through the set of doors from the lobby to the rink opening and stopped at the four inch drop to the ice. The scene in front of me was a blur of commotion. I smelled the remnants of propane from the Zamboni. I saw my breath swirl about me in the cold air.

I took off my gloves to snap up my chin strap. It took several moments as my fingers did not respond because of the cold and numbness. It took both hands and all my fingers and thumbs to finally snap the strap to the other side of my helmet.

Making sure it was secure, I put my gloves back on, took a deep breath, looked left and right and stepped onto the shiny surface. I'd been playing hockey before Wayne Gretzky was born and I hoped four decades of programming would rescue me. I thought skating was like riding a bike *Once you learn, you never forget, right?*

Wrong.

I put my left skate onto the ice and pushed with my right. My legs forgot the programming. I slowly sank to the ice. Like a balloon being deflated, they crumpled, and seconds later I was on my knees.

Dozens of blades belonging to kids and parents flashed by me. Humiliated, I shuffled on my knees to the boards, an arm's length away. I struggled to pull myself up against the wall. My arms had the same strength as my legs. Panting, I stood on my shaky skates. I looked at the arena clock. 8:14.

I vowed to skate until the bottom of the hour. Again, I pushed off, staying only inches away from the boards, my right glove sliding along the striker near the Plexiglas. I found myself concentrating, *left stride, right stride, left stride, right stride*...I had to consciously put one skate in front of the other.

As I had my head down, looking at them and counting my cadence, a youngster ran into me from behind. We both tumbled like pins in a bowling alley. He mumbled an inaudible apology.

Fifteen minutes later and sweating profusely, I was skating better. My legs were still rubbery, but I hadn't fallen. *Five more minutes* I told myself. Three more times around the circumference of the rink and I headed for the doors to the lobby. I stumbled onto the solid footing. Trembling, sore and out of breath, I fell back onto the bench where I'd left my sneakers.

I couldn't believe it. I was back on the blades. I'd overcome the first major hurdle in my dream to play hockey again. My shaking fingers untied my laces and pulled the wet skates from my feet. When I stood up in my runners I felt as if I'd just stepped from a boat. I packed everything into my bag, slung it over my shoulder and left the rink.

Light snow was falling from the overcast skies with about an inch on the ground. I still had my sea legs when I got to the car.

I could hear my joints snap as I sat behind the wheel. I turned on the dome light and looked in the rear-view mirror. My cheeks were beet red. Steam rose from my head and my drenched short hair was glued to my scalp. I could see the outline of the helmet where it sat on my forehead. One of the motivations to get back skating was an invitation by my brother to play in their annual father-son game in Salmon Arm just before Christmas. I had three weeks to get into shape. We had planned to celebrate Christmas in Calgary because Caroline's sister and husband, Connie and Doug Florence, were flying in from Australia. We only saw them once every four years.

I skated each weekday afternoon from noon to 1 p.m. at Memorial Arena for the daily adult skate and on the last Tuesday before the holiday break, I was skating strongly, but hadn't quite reached the smooth, graceful form before cancer. I also noted my body was slowly starting to return to it's pre-chemotherapy shape, Even though my stomach was still flabby, it was decreasing in size.

On December 21st, two days before we left for Salmon Arm, I became a born-again hockey player. The nerves I felt three weeks earlier, were nothing like I experienced in the old dressing room for the noon hour old-timers hockey game. My stomach was churning.

The moths had morphed into eagles.

When I lugged my equipment bag into the room, my head began to swim. Forty years of hockey sights, sounds, smells and emotions surfaced. I was introduced to the others by Herb Clapham, the organizer of the noon hour ritual. He knew of my cancer battle, as he was a manager at the bank where Caroline worked.

The night before, I had carefully packed my bag, making sure I hadn't forgotten anything. I had mentally dressed and undressed myself several times before I zipped it up.

As the room filled up with guys dragging in their hockey bags, I laid my equipment on the floor in front of me, like I'd done thousands of times before. It all seemed so strange, all of a sudden. It was like I was getting dressed for the first time. I had to think about where all my protective gear went into place on my body. It was like I needed a manual but I did know one thing for sure. The protective cup was the first to be put on.

I was sweating by the time I reached for my shoulder pads, the last piece of equipment to go into place. It had taken much longer than I remembered. I finally drew the jersey over my head and winced when a shot of pain rifled through my left shoulder. I took ten minutes to limber up, stretching my groin, shoulders and back. I was hurting and I had yet to step on the ice. *This is not good* I thought.

I bent over to pick to pick up my helmet. For a moment, before I placed it on my head, I paused and stared at it. I had never noticed the nicks and marks caused by sticks, pucks and tape from combat over the fifteen years since I bought it. The visor was also well scratched. *Boy, if this thing could talk.*

I'd played in hundreds of industrial league contests and participated in countless charity hockey games in rural rinks for the radio station where I worked in southern Alberta. In some of the contests, we raised money for terminally ill patients and their families.

How ironic it was that I was skating in a game, meaningless to everyone but me.

It was part of my healing, my therapy, my life. I put on the old lid, snapped up the strap, with difficulty again, put on my gloves, grabbed my stick at the door and followed the guys on the fifty foot walk to the ice. As I stepped down to it, I lurched forward, my stick cutting the air like a scythe.

After a five minute warm-up, I skated to the bench and sat down. Before I knew it, the game started. I leaned forward, itching to hop over the boards like I used to and get into the play. My nerves were raw and tingling. The shouts, the sound of the puck careening off the boards echoed into the concrete wall behind the bench. I heard the whack of sticks taking a pass, the slicing of hard steel on cold ice, the cheers and laughter. It was deliriously delicious.

I was jolted to reality when a gloved hand gave me a smack on my right shoulder pad and an excited voice said, "you're on, get going" I bolted through the narrow door.

Striding as hard as I could, I zeroed in on the puck. I didn't touch it on my first shift, my second or third. I did a lot of chasing the guy with the puck however.

Next time, I promised myself.

Slowly, shift by shift, I got stronger and my skating improved with each thrust of my legs. The endorphins had kicked in and the pain I had at the beginning was gone. I finally got to handle the puck and even scored an easy goal with less than 10 minutes to go. I simply flipped the puck into the open net when the goalie had gone down after making the initial save on a shot from the blue line by one of our defencemen.

Like that afternoon in the spring when I held my shovel high, my stick was pointed to the rafters.

After the game as I sat in my soaked equipment, Herb came over and congratulated me. None of the others knew of my chemotherapy. I took my equipment off slowly, savoring every moment. Some of the guys had to get back to work so they quickly showered, got dressed and left. Steam circulated through the musty room as laughter ricocheted around the walls. I had taken it all for granted in the past.

When most of them had left, I walked across the room and gingerly stepped into the shower under a stream of hot water. My toes were still very cold and I stifled a cry of pain. It felt as if a million tiny needles were splashing on them but at the same time, it felt so very good. I didn't know how long I stood in the shower stall but when I finished, the dressing room was empty. I toweled off, sat down on the bench where my clothes were hanging and slowly got dressed.

I breathed in deeply and slumped backward onto the cold wall. Raw, male sweat permeated the room. I inhaled the odor from ancient shin and shoulder pads, unwashed underwear and liniment. My eyes scanned the room slowly, stopping to rest on scattered remnants of broken hockey sticks, discarded sock tape and empty pop and beer cans.

There was water everywhere.

A well-used puck with chips hacked from it's edges rested

on end beside the garbage can a couple of feet away from me. *You're a wounded warrior, aren't you* I thought as I reached over and picked it up. *How many times have you been pounded off the boards and picked out of a net?*

The sight clouded my eyes. It was like a dream. Was I really out there? Did I really skate and score again?

I stood up and groaned. Yep. The pain had returned. I gathered up my drenched equipment and jammed them into my hockey bag. With difficulty, I swung it over my shoulder and grabbed my sticks. *Holy mackerel, I forgot how heavy this stuff is.*

I paused and looked back when I got to the open door and smiled.

The following day we left for my brother's place in Salmon Arm and that night for the first time in 32 years Wolf and I played hockey together, and to make it even more special, our sons skated with us on the same side. Chris and I had teamed up together many times in the past when I was one of his minor hockey coaches. That night, brothers and cousins had joined forces. To add icing on the cake, each of us scored two goals.

In the dressing room after the game, I marvelled at how things had changed as we began to take off our gear. Wolf brought back two cans each of pop and beer. He gave a brew to Ryan and Chris while he and I had a Pepsi.

> *Journal entry: Christmas 1994 in Calgary. I was surprised at how calm I am. I thought I might be more emotional. I shed a few tears when I saw my family and friends, but on the whole, I sat back and reflected. I tried to put it all in perspective. Thinking, rationalizing and analyzing. One thought alone surfaced repeatedly. I'M ALIVE! I'M HERE WITH THOSE I LOVE. NOTHING ELSE MATTERS!*

We headed back to Penticton on the 27th of December, eyes dry, emotions brimming and the trunk of the car full of goodies.

Four days later, Chris, Jodi and I were back on the Trans Canada Highway through the mountains of snow at the Roger's Pass on the way to Calgary again. Caroline's mother had passed away on New Year's Day 1995. She'd been suffering from Alzheimer's disease for more than a decade. Earlier that day, we'd raced to get Caroline to a plane in Kelowna for a flight to Calgary. She made it in time to be with her mother when she passed away.

At the funeral, we gathered again with our extended family. I sat with Caroline and the kids as we looked ahead at the coffin in the funeral chapel. I thought back to my cancer experience and let the scene unfold in front of me.

Back home a couple of days later, I celebrated the new year by accepting a job with the sales team at Skaha Ford. I knew the teasing would start from my gear-head friends who knew I'd been refurbishing Chevs all my life. I rationalized that selling Fords would do many things for me, including paying off the mortgage, saving for RRSP's again, buying food and restoring my old '62.

I was on my feet eight hours a day in the showroom and on the new and used car lot. My legs were sore for a couple of weeks but I soon became used to the pace. My hair had also fully grown back. It felt good to run a brush through it again.

I played hockey twice a week on two different teams. By the end of January, I had almost reached my pre-cancer level of fitness. I also realized I was having fun like never before. I had taken my recreational hockey much too seriously in the past and found myself uptight before each game and berated myself if I missed a scoring chance.

Not any more. I was loosey-goosey each time I hit the ice. Because I was enjoying it more, I was playing better, skating faster and shooting harder. My attitude had changed. One

Friday night in March, I scored six times on a goalie twenty years younger than I was.

I could also not shake the image of Ironman and those sights and sounds from the previous August played out in my mind constantly. Each time I suited up for hockey, I remembered how ill and weak I was when we first witnessed the event.

Is it possible that I...could...finish...it?

My sixth month checkup was scheduled for early April in Vancouver. Before I left, I took a few cassettes with me, including the greatest hits of Roy Orbison.

"No evidence of cancer" was Dr. Fairey's verdict.

As I streaked home at 70 miles an hour, I cranked up the volume of my favorite Orbison tape. I was 12 years old when I first heard Roy's voice and over the decades, through marriage, kids, cars, jobs, cities and cancer, his voice was incorporated into the mosaic of my life. When I was sad, he was sad with me. Melancholy moments heard us sing "In Dreams", "Crying", I'm Hurtin'" and "Blue Bayou" in unison.

In happy times, we sang, "Candy Man" and "Pretty Woman".

I hit the window switch to open it. I leaned my head out and felt the wind blast thought my hair. It felt wonderful. The budding spring beauty of the Fraser Valley unfolded in front of me as the ribbon of asphalt rolled under the Buick. Leaves had sprouted in the trees and everywhere, nature was renewing itself.

As I shot over the bridges and miles of highway, I turned up the level of the cassette even higher to overcome the road noise. I sang loud and lustily with all the gusto I could force from my once-again healthy lungs.

People in cars to my left who passed gave me strange looks but I didn't care. I hit all the high notes on "Only The Lonely" never missing a beat.

To this day, I'm certain that somewhere, wherever heaven

is, Roy was singing with me and smiling, his eyes twinkling behind his famous black sunglasses.

"…..OOOoooOOOHHHH, PRETTY WOMAN!"

Back on the ice again, healthy and fit.

Order Form

Books and videos available from *Circle Of Light Publishing.*

Through The Valley Of The Shadow	$18.50
From Hodgkin's To Ironman	$15.00
Both books	$30.00
Video – *From Hodgkin's To Ironman*	$25.00

Please Note: taxes, shipping and handling
are <u>included</u> in the above

To download order form, go to: www.wallyhild.com

Or, send cheque or money order to:

Circle Of Light Publishing
2636 Roblin Street
Penticton, BC, Canada
V2A 6H4

Please mail me:

__copy(ies) Through The Valley Of The Shadow   total_____

__copy(ies) From Hodgkin's To Ironman   total_____

__both   total_____

__copy(ies) Video – From Hodgkin's To Ironman   total_____

Name _____

Address _____

Country _____   PC/Zip _____

Phone _____   email _____

ISBN 141207556-4